WHERE THE WIND BEGINS

By the same author:
Song for Sarah

Stories of Hurting People
Who Said Yes to Life

A SEQUEL TO *SONG FOR SARAH*

WHERE THE WIND BEGINS

PAULA D'ARCY

Harold Shaw Publishers
Wheaton, Illinois

Acknowledgment is made for use of the following copyrighted material:

"Wind on the Hill," on page 9 from *Now We Are Six* by A. A. Milne, used by permission of E. P. Dutton.

The section of the poem "Behind The Walls" on page 125 is reprinted from *The Secret Trees* by Luci Shaw by permission of Harold Shaw Publishers. Copyright © 1976 by Luci Shaw.

The poem "Judas, Peter" on page 126 is reprinted from *The Sighting* by Luci Shaw by permission of Harold Shaw Publishers. Copyright © 1981 by Luci Shaw.

"It Was God's Will," pages 130-132 by Sheldon Vanauken is reprinted by permission of *The Living Church*, 407 East Michigan St., Milwaukee, Wis. 53202.

The poem "Pneuma" on pages 142-143 is reprinted from *The Secret Trees* by Luci Shaw by permission of Harold Shaw Publishers. Copyright © 1976 by Luci Shaw.

Cover photo: Robert McKendrick

ISBN 0-87788-925-2

Printed in the United States of America

Library of Congress Cataloging in Publication Data

D'Arcy, Paula, 1947-
    Where the wind begins.

    1. D'Arcy, Paula, 1947-   .   2. Christian biography—
United States.   3. Christian life—1960-   .   I. Title.
BR1725.D34A39   1984   248.4   84-1313
ISBN 0-87788-923-6

5   4   3   2   1   94   93   92   91   90   89   88   87   86   85

To Ken Harper
who in his deep, painful search
for truth asked me the questions
which became this book.

Contents

WIND ON THE HILL

No one can tell me,
    Nobody knows,
Where the wind comes from
    Where the wind goes.

It's flying from somewhere
    As fast as it can,
I couldn't keep up with it,
    Not if I ran.

But if I stopped holding
    The string of my kite,
It would blow with the wind
    For a day and a night.

And then when I found it,
    Wherever it blew,
I should know that the wind
    Had been going there too.

So then I could tell them
    Where the wind goes . . .
But where the wind comes from
    Nobody knows.

A. A. Milne

FOREWORD

As I sit writing, settled comfortably into my faded, child-worn sofa, thin ribbons of wind howl through the spaces and cracks around the window across the living room from me. Outside on the lawn snow-covered maples and oaks bend and dance, occasionally reaching to tap icy notes onto the pane. There is a furious rhythm in their cadence, and the force of the wind is frightening. With each wailing gust it seems chillier inside.

Beth is curled up beside me, alternately watching the disciplined motions of my pen across a yellow-lined legal pad and the seeming chaos of the storm. She pushes closer for warmth and then asks, "Mommy, where does the wind begin?"—a childish question, asked as easily as, "Where have you put my clean socks?"

But her question, though childish, is not trivial, for her wondering really reaches into mystery, the realm of questions without complete answers—life which defies easy prediction or containment, life which we can never entirely measure or understand. And strangely it is in the heart of life's mystery, in the web of seeming contradiction and betrayed expectation, that truth and freedom really lie.

INTRODUCTION

Song for Sarah is the journal which records my 1973 marriage to Roy D'Arcy, the birth of our first daughter, Sarah, and the 1975 car accident involving a drunken driver which took Roy and Sarah's lives and shattered my perfect world. Three months pregnant at the time, I struggled painfully to face these deaths and to accept my changed life. I reached for something immovable, and found God.

After *Song for Sarah* was published I was invited to appear on many talk shows, so I have some idea of the kinds of questions interviewers ask and the things they want to know. As I pull the pages of this book, one by one from the typewriter, I am convinced that no interviewer will be able to resist asking me, "Where *does* the wind begin?"

But how can I tell them? My answer for that belongs only to me. And your answer belongs to you. And if that's more mystery than you like, then these accounts of mystery, contradiction, and "truth found in unexpected places" are for someone else.

Sometimes I feel that God is writing this book on my heart, but he's leaving it to me to pull it out and put it down in words on paper. It's a hurtful process. I wish it were otherwise. But then, I say that about life just about every other day.

Life hurts when it tricks me, and I am just beginning to catch on to some of its wiles. I will never be fooled again into thinking that it is a series of absolutes. It isn't. It is not shocking *National Enquirer* headlines. It is neither total happiness nor constant tears. It is neither bliss nor despair. It is not black or white anything.

You will read this in a hundred different ways in the pages to follow: Life comes at us all at once—everything together. It is the middle ground, as well as the extremes. It is separate people being many things at once. It is ongoing possibility and constant change. And life is subject, like nothing else, to our expectations. If we think it static or rigid we'll have it just that way. That's why it matters to see it as the limitless gift that it is.

Can life really be happy? I think so. But happiness is not a time or place. It is not a continuum, nor a condition, and it doesn't have fixed spatial qualities such as length. Sometimes it may only be caught for a moment, and yet we know it is real. Its secret is that it lives inside us, requiring our inner involvement, not dependent upon special circumstances in the outside world. Wherever it lives, the outside ceases to matter. Happiness can be any color, any shade, any degree.

When we start separating qualities like happiness from their polar opposites, such as sadness, we are meddling in peripheral things and missing the fact that *all* qualities stir around together within us, and need to. We hide behind well-practiced defenses and think we are shielding ourselves from hurt. We believe that by denying fear we can avoid being scared, or feeling vulnerable. We think that if we don't cry on the outside then we aren't crying. But that's not so; we merely end up living our real lives on the inside where no one sees. And after a while neither do we see. We become unable to find ourselves.

In time we are very lost. We are people who have

wandered so far from the persons we were born to be
that we distance ourselves from ever finding where joy
really lies. Is it sinful to walk away, on the inside, from
the life we've been given? To be afraid to love and be
who we are? To feel and know? Are there many of us
who look very much in place but who are really among
the missing?

And what's the antidote? Perhaps it's found in allowing life. Accepting it. Feeling it. Facing it. Letting it
be. I love Russell Hoban's line in *Turtle Diary* which
says, "I am the single enemy of my freedom."[1] How
right I have discovered this to be. Life's fullness often
sits idle in our own hands.

Be glad that life is mysterious and stop setting boundaries as if you could make it otherwise. Consider that
an unpredictable life need not be feared. Imagine that
behind *all* its diverse faces life is wonderful. And don't
limit it by any of the narrow expectations you have
learned. Start unlearning them. Throw them away.

Dare to believe that in all terror is goodness, in all
sadness, joy. And vice versa, too. Dare to look at life
and people and heartache and God in a new way. Dare
to think that all of the anticipated ways may not actually
be the only ways love is trying to enter your life. Dare to
believe that you can cross the manmade boundaries.
Dare to think about how it would feel not to be trapped
in your own prison of safety. Instead drink fully of life
and people and places. This is your day. Life is the gift.
And it is good. (Genesis 1:31)

1
THE VILLAGE
UNDER THE
BED

Let me take refuge
in the shelter
of thy wings.
Psalm 61:4

ONCE, WHEN BETH WAS FOUR, we unwillingly booked passage on a voyage all mothers dread. Our tickets read: *Destination:* A Winter of Constant Childhood Sickness. December, January, and February sailed past Beth's dormer window without our being able to be outside. Our calendar of the passing days became neat finger strokes drawn in the wood-framed slate our hot breath made on the window pane. Together we became weather reporters, announcing the changing elements as they appeared in our square of glass. And at times I thought I'd grow old at that window, and imagined myself with long, grey braids and a wrinkled frame, still carrying thermometers, aspirin, and glasses of juice to a middle-aged Beth.

But aside from such snatches of despair, we were mostly cheery and cozy inside. The slanted ceiling of Beth's bedroom lends it a storybook air, as do the stuffed ducks, turtles, and bears which hang from the ceiling in proud array. And atop Beth's bureau, and peeking from every shelf, are more fuzzy animals and big, lovable rag dolls.

Only Beth's bed interrupted the fairy tale feeling, for around it I had been forced to build a strange looking contraption. Two sets of skis (a ski to each bed post) supported a vast pavilion of sheets which created the steam tent in which Beth's chronic croup forced her to live. It was, if I do say so, quite an elegant affair, almost as though custom-designed and erected by Neiman Marcus.

With my head poking inside this "mist city" I said to Beth, "Let's pretend it's a great adventure!" So we decorated the humidifier with colored stickers and sat Barbie dolls at each of the four corners. Paper dolls paraded up and down the sheets. Stacks of Golden Books were our fortress against possible invasion, and a fleet of matchbox cars and trucks serviced our Department of the Interior.

To Beth's credit, she rarely complained about her confinement. She accepted her substandard housing with a good measure of tolerance, and only occasionally asked me to describe the rest of our house so she'd remember it. And though I tired quickly from the nighttime bouts of her coughing and wheezing, she never seemed to be without pep and a smile. Her joy was an incentive. It often buoyed the nurse.

But all things will eventually end. Someone once said that. And they must have known. And when you are nursing a sick child, looking up "sleeping through the whole night" in a reference volume to refresh yourself on its meaning, you cling to that motto that "All Things Eventually End." When they did, it was with real celebration.

Spring came. My friend Stuart arrived sympathetically at the door one morning with a bouquet of daffodils. They colored my day. And with spring's warmth came health. The doctor pronounced Beth *cured*.

Gratefully I set myself to the task of cleaning, and tearing down. Anticipating Beth's joy at release, I was totally unprepared for her burst of tears. She begged me to leave the steam tent intact; she couldn't believe I would be so merciless and destructive about it, for it had become her own kingdom, trespassed by no one.

Several times I'd been a visitor to her shores, even allowed to sit inside with my gifts of tea cakes and juices as a teller of stories or a singer of songs. But mostly this had been Beth's territory and it hurt her to see it go.

I think I understood, for how few are the things children really rule! How magnificent it must have been to her to have had charge, even at the expense of sickness, of a little kingdom!

I felt like "Mother the Monster." But the dirt and crumbs were so embedded that cleaning just had to be carried out. Everything washable was washed, everything sweepable was swept. Beth used up two bottles of Windex and mountains of paper towels as she polished her way around the walls.

I felt powerful. Symbolically I had killed every germ. I had washed away winter and splashed on spring.

Eventually Beth wandered off downstairs in search of more glass to polish, and I rolled up her braided rug and began shoving and pushing all the furniture to the center of the floor. I strained against the dead weight of the bed. I knew I should wait for a neighbor to help, but I managed it with one last push. There. Rags and ammonia in hand, I knelt to scrub the hardwood boards. And I could not believe my eyes.

All around the room lay the bare, dusty hardwood floor, brown-stained boards everywhere waiting for my touch. *Almost* everywhere, for as I stared incredulously at the patch of floor which had been beneath Beth's bed, I was looking at an unbelievable scene. Faces and buildings were staring back at me, each sketched in bold magic marker in purples, reds, yellows, blues—rectangular mouths, squat bodies, shapes of delight and abandon, skyscrapers, tiny dwellings. Stunned, I exclaimed, "I can't believe it—there's a village of people beneath this bed!"

Then that regrettable parent part of me, the part which has grown up a little, fairly groaned, "My hardwood floors!" Were they ruined? Would the marks come off? I wanted to cry. Cautiously I dabbed a little ammonia and cleanser onto a colored line. Relief. I could make it disappear.

I kept working away. I was nearly done when the part of me which probably will never grow up suddenly stopped my hand. What was I doing? I was erasing a treasure. I was weighing the value of a floor against the worth of a dream, and the floor was winning.

I stopped right there.

Carefully I cleaned every other inch of that room, but preserved the remaining lines of the village scene. My priorities back in order, I tended it with great care, and I looked a long while before I pushed the bed back into place. To my newly-opened eyes that stretch of floor was very beautiful.

It was many weeks later before I questioned Beth about the drawings. "Oh," she grinned, "they kept me company while I was sick, and they scared away the monsters so I'd be safe."

Yes.

Grownups have their own monsters, their own villages. Our monsters all belong to the genus of *fear*—fear of failure, fear of commitment, fear of loving and being loved, fear of ridicule, fear of loss, fear of not being as

successful as society, or our own expectations, say we
ought to be.

And every fear limits our expectations. We begin to
believe less. We dare to hope for less. We confine our
hearts (and minds) only to possibilities which are safe
and reasonable. Sadly the resulting villages of protection we create are inked, often indelibly, inside our own
hearts.

I receive countless letters telling me about the monsters in people's lives. Again and again people feel
defeated by the things which happen to them and their
resulting fear of the future. Beth's village was her way
of coping with what seemed scary and unknown,
making it manageable. But is there a solution for us? I
think so, and it's not far removed from Beth's imaginary
land, for it has to do with *trust*. Being able to dream and
create and being able to trust are related.

Overcoming comes from within. And its cornerstone
is a trust in the ongoing goodness and possibility in all
life.

The old saying is true. If you want sure defeat, then
believe that things can't change. Convince yourself that
there is no hope. Identify yourself with all the elements
of your failed situation. Say to yourself, "This effort is a
failure, therefore I am a failure. This hasn't worked out,
therefore I am worthless. This reality is miserable, so I
will be miserable." But what is defeating is not the situation. It is believing it.

But if you want sure victory, then believe that things
can change. Learn to move beyond your failed endeav-
ors. Say to yourself, "This may have been wrong; I may

even have been at fault, but I can learn and change. The situation showed me my inadequacy, but also where to go to reinforce my strengths." For God and you, together, are greater than any circumstance. The victory is in that belief.

Dreams and hopes are not childish, nor are they silly. They are really the faith-language by which our souls translate their visions. But only we can free them.

Every day we decide whether or not to risk searching for the person God created, and the dream with which that person was imbued. Our monsters are whoever or whatever attempts to dissuade us from this course. They are all the ruses which work to convince us that life is not good and should not be celebrated. That our life does not matter. That anything is insignificant. They are the faces and circumstances which say that the dream will never be.

And whether or not to trust and pursue the dream is the soul's dilemma.

2
SEARCHING
FOR
MYSELF

*... it is neither the coming or the
going that is of consequence—
what is of consequence is the
beauty that one gathers in
this interlude called life.*
Winston O. Abbott,
Come Walk Among the Stars

SOMEONE ONCE SAID that when grief picks us up it never puts us down again in the same spot. We move. We change. We are all that we were before, plus the experience which has hurt us, plus the new individual who emerges to cope, and to move on. And so our neat and predictable little lives become our past, and our present is always expanding in new directions.

I might have predicted that I, over-anxious, fearing another loss, would smother Beth, but I have found that I am freer with her than I ever was with her sister, Sarah. I learned something very important through the death of my husband and first child. Nothing in life can ultimately be controlled by me. All is free. And when life is held lightly, as intended, it grows in beauty and fascination.

Probably one of my most frequently asked questions concerns how I have adjusted to single life. Are you lonely? people inquire. Are you sad? Do you think you'll remarry? Isn't it hard being the single parent of an only child?

I usually wince at these questions, thinking, Here we go again! And even as I write this there is a temptation to be less than honest. To simply report that by now everything is okay. But in reality it was a hard-won fight to get to today's "okay."

Being single is seldom a chosen role. More often it is an unwanted reality, and for as long as it continues it can remain an unappreciated gift. It feels more like something to be endured.

And it is precisely this ingrained attitude which causes the single state to test even a strong individual's

best resources. I never guessed that I carried such convictions about the "rightness" of being part of a two-
some. But when an accident changed the dream of my
life, it exposed those words, written there quite clearly.

At twenty-seven I was a happy wife and mother. My
husband and my not-quite-two-year-old daughter defined my world. A second child was on the way. It was
all close to perfect.

Then—hard reality. On Friday I was a married
woman. On Saturday I was a widow. Single. And life
had to be started all over again at a new place. When the
single adult looks into the night, he looks alone.

In my early widowhood I became skilled at reminding
myself how apart, how alone I really was. In hundreds
of small ways I convinced myself that life was an ex-
clusive club to which I no longer belonged. And that
negative set of my mind, that conviction that to be
single was to be a loser, made me thoroughly unhappy
and uncomfortable most of the time. Marriage, I just
knew, made life right; singleness made life wretched.

One September afternoon I walked several miles
along a deserted stretch of beach I'd grown to love. I
kicked at stones along the water's edge and absent-
mindedly watched as the waves covered the blue and
red straps of my worn beach thongs. I'd come looking
for answers to my hated aloneness.

I finally settled into a niche against the sea wall and
idly watched a grey gull pick at crab shells the tide had
washed ashore. My right hand dug around for stones
and shells, and finding one I made half-hearted furrows
in the damp sand.

There weren't any answers. And after a while my

mind wandered to another beach, several years earlier, where I'd collected smooth stones with a chattering, red-haired eleven-year-old boy named Scott. I was then in graduate school, studying to be a counselor. As part of a required practicum, each candidate had to counsel several clients in a small, square, green-rugged room which was backed with a large two-way mirror. As each aspiring counselor sat in fierce concentration, hoping to respond with the right word at the right time, our class-mates and professors, unseen behind the mirror, sat scribbling observations. Later on, our handling of the session would be the subject of intense classroom re-view.

Clients for such interviews were understandably dif-ficult to find. For a counselee it was a bit like yielding one's wounded body into the hands of a fledgling phy-sician. Most people were reluctant to serve science at such possible risk.

Thus, when a prospective client was announced in class, we all eagerly bid for the opportunity to work with him or her. But the day our professor told us about an angry, nonconforming eleven-year-old boy, there was silence. I knew the other students were thinking my thoughts. An eleven-year-old boy? Who knew any-thing about kids? Where would you begin? What would you say? Much better to stick with adults who would appreciate and respond to philosophy and theory.

When no one seemed interested in Scott, the pro-fessor finally announced, "Well, if no one will speak up, I will. Paula, I am assigning this case to you." My heart sank into my stomach. Dread.

When I first met Scott, he was as noncommunicative

and uncooperative as I'd feared. He defied me to be nice to him, conveying that impression by the look in his eyes and the set of his jaw. While his parents pleasantly outlined his school misbehaviors and some general problems with anger, he stood defiantly by the door. He never spoke, nor did he say good-bye when they left.

For six agonizing weeks Scott's parents brought him to the college for his weekly appointment. I had him captive for an hour, but that was all. He was determined to keep me from penetrating his world.

When I'd run out of words to say we sometimes squared off and sat in silence. Finally, at a classmate's suggestion I struggled to get involved with him in a joint project; for two sessions we dutifully and silently strung green beads onto elastic thread, making the "hippie" strands which were so popular then, in the sixties. It was tough to decide which one of us hated it more.

After the fourth or fifth week I'd begun not to care about my practicum, my grade, or my performance. What I did care about deeply was reaching this boy, yet I hadn't a clue, not one idea as to how to reach him and motivate him to let me in.

At the end of six weeks I went to my professor in despair, and begged him to let me "counsel" Scott in my own way. I knew I needed to be his friend and gain his trust. I also knew it would never happen in that sterile cubicle. My professor listened, and finally agreed.

So the following week, and for weeks thereafer, Scott and I spent our hour together walking. We walked through beautiful parts of my New Hampshire campus and visited the university farm, following narrow trails which forked through the dense green woods. We walked winter into spring.

Initially Scott continued to mistrust my motives, and was wary and defensive most of the time. For a long while I didn't talk at all. But by nods and short syllables we eventually began communicating with one another, commenting on the natural world which surrounded us. Little by little we became rather fond buddies, our companionship being that of two travelers exploring a new realm together. In time, Scott haltingly shared with me some of his fears, and let me glimpse some of the vulnerable places he had kept so well protected. The friendship grew, and with it more dialogue. The realm we were exploring was, I suppose, his heart. And mine.

One day we walked along the beach near his home, collecting smooth stones. And the last day that we were together we had a race in the rain.

I never said anything profound to Scott, at least not that I know of. But I believed in him so strongly. He stood apart, but in a beautiful way. The one thing I remember was that I assured him that there can be rightness in things which are different from the norm. I said, "Be you."

And now, years later, I scraped those two words into the sand. *Be you.*

Really the normalcy, the sense of rightness I was seeking, that we all seek, is found when we find God and know we belong to him. The key is not to expect from other people the fulfillment that only God can be.

I know I'm somehow always feeling guilty about becoming new in some way. I wonder if "they" will like it,
or me. And so in effect I have too often handed over my
life to all of "them" and relinquished control. Only my
foolishness convinces me that this happened because of
outside forces. Deep down I know it happens because
of me.

And as I struggle to simplify my life, I begin to know
myself better. That isn't possible when I am burying
myself with busyness or throwing myself away into
everyone else's demands and activities. When I am left
with some time for myself I can sort out the parts of
me that I don't ever want to compromise because they
are the core of who I am.

So it is okay to stand alone. It is okay to be one. It
is okay to be me.

In fact, that's the point: that I become the one God
has created me to be. I focus on that daily, and it's hard,
so that I fail in that daily, too. But superceding all that
I am, and all of my struggle, is my awareness of his
presence at the center of all things, including me. And I
know that when I give this struggle to be myself to him,
he works more efficiently within me. He refines me.
He enhances my real self. And he knows that as I give
myself first to his service, he will be able to hand my self
back to me, more whole than before.

That is denial and becoming, the way of negation and
the way of affirmation, all in one breath. But it's for
him, not me. That's the difference.

Slowly I am coming to realize that love may come in
many forms. Love need not be defined "husband." It
comes with many faces. Some are pretenders—rela-

tionships and feelings which call themselves love, but are not, for they make impossible demands and deny us the self which is God's gift. But some are real and we must be alert to recognize them. It is an ongoing struggle; maybe I won't always know what love is. But I hope I'll learn to recognize what it isn't.

It is true that when one is single there seems to be less to hold on to. The root system of "family" is often not there. There is no one else to lean against, no buffer. I have often lamented, "When life meets me, I'm on my own."

But I've come to see that my empty hands may not be such a disadvantage at all. Perhaps they keep me a little closer than most to the truth that everything is passing, that roots are deceptive.

Maybe some wisdom lies in the words I remember hurling at God during a moment of hurt and despair. I angrily told him, "Now I have no one to lean on but you." And he said, "Exactly."

I struggle to keep believing. But when I am ready to despair I remember that "My soul follows hard after thee: thy right hand upholds me."[2]

And then I stretch out my hand to the new day. It is grasped. "I will never leave you," he says.

These words were first spoken to men who had given up their families and friends. In my singleness, I can sense their sorrow. But in Christ's companionship, I also can share their calling.

The apostles seem rather set apart, chosen men who actually walked with the man Jesus. But, two thousand years later, we are all equally called.

What uncomfortable knowledge! It *demands* some-

thing of me, if I really hear it. I know the usual arguments (rebuttals?): Actually, I like my life the way it's
going. Ups and downs, sure. Struggles. But also satis-
factions. Mastery. Decision-making. Control. I like
having autonomy. I fear what following Jesus may
demand. Being alone may have its problems, but being
with him is really risky.

Oh, I am willing to believe in him and meet him in
church. In a crisis I'll gladly call on him. But what if he
interferes with the comfortable network I've built
around me? What if he makes me responsible for living
up to certain standards? What if he interferes with my
pleasures? What if he's always pricking my conscience
with his wisdom? He's given me this life, so why can't I
do with it as I please?

Is that so wrong? I love my family and I'm hurting
no one. My life is good and decent and that should be
enough. Anything more is for fanatics. Period.

The sensible conclusion is that not everybody should
have to take this Christ so seriously. It should be okay
to simply lead your life in your own way. In the end the
notion that someone was "calling" me won't make one
bit of difference.

Unless it is the truth.

What if it is? What if my name is really being called?
Faith in God, faith in a *great* God may be a wonderful
thing, but what if it's only a mental assent? If it's not
followed with the actual commitment of legs, arms, and
heart, is it like the proverbial hidden talent—a life not
being what it was meant to be? Or could be?

Taking the step is hard. How does God the *concept*—

God the *topic* they'd laugh at me for mentioning over cocktails—become God the *person* in my everyday life? Do I dare believe that my life could be utterly different —*better*—following him?

So, just for the sake of conversation, say he *is* the truth and say that—unknown to anyone who'd laugh— I had said "Come into my heart and show me the real meaning of this crazy life"—if I *did* say that, what would happen?

Here's what happened to me.

I first followed truth into the world of publishing. I never set out to write a book; a book happened to me. I thought with panic of my most intimate memories rolling over and over, inking their way through large presses onto 7" x 9" pieces of heavy white paper, of my life being bound. "Use it," I said, "if you will." But whatever for?

When I first walked past bookstores which displayed me I ducked. This was not my idea. What on earth did God intend to do? I wasn't sure I liked this at all. *He* was the right decision. But perhaps this wasn't. Did the signals get crossed?

It was a long while before the momentum quickened. And I was so involved in my life's small details that I failed to see that the hand of God was always gently guiding me in a purposeful direction.

By December of 1980, following the *Reader's Digest* condensation of *Song for Sarah*, shopping bags of mail clogged my kitchen floor. Some who wrote were merely seeking assurance: Are you all right? Are you happy now? Will you be okay? And I couldn't imagine what inspired so many wonderful strangers to write.

I'd thought that the story of a mother losing a child was going to touch only other mothers who'd lost a child. How was I to account for all these bundles of mail from men? They told me they were writing from their offices so no one would know. Sheepishly they confessed, "I cried when I read your story. Men aren't supposed to admit loneliness and be afraid. But I'm both."

Unexpectedly I found that the most representative letter told me, "After reading your traumatic story I realize how very lucky I am... How blessed to have a wonderful family. I think your story will help me list my priorities and give me new direction. I know I must make more time for us, our family, our love."

I sat stunned. I had never expected that my pain would help someone else to realize what they had while they had it. It made me so grateful for deciding to publish. Those lives told me it was worth it.

And how easy it was, in pain, to feel that I had a corner on suffering. Letter after letter proved me wrong —I couldn't believe the tragedies. Parents and siblings all lost in a plane crash, returning from a young girl's wedding. Two teen-agers in a family committing suicide six months apart. Intolerable, unrelenting emotional and physical pain. Then two haunting lines which to me were the saddest of all:

"When there was time I never showed my love.

Now it's too late."

As I focussed on these lives, Christ was continually instructing me.

I understood as never before that the ongoing mission of love is dependent upon people. When someone prays, other people are often the answer. And when people are unwilling to get involved, there's silence. The interconnectedness of all living things is both beautiful and frightening. We weren't called to be comfortable. We were called to be involved. We were called to serve.

One day in 1980 I was called by Dr. Norman Vincent Peale with a request to address a school of ministers gathered for renewal in Pawling, New York. Such a request seemed so incredible that there wasn't even space for an argument. How could I ever do it? Public speaking would have been my very last choice of service, following behind hard labor.

I stood with Moses. "Not this assignment, God. Send someone else. This I cannot do." I'd spent high school and college avoiding speech classes and oral presentations. "Anything else, but not this."

I pled without result. And deep within me an awareness began to grow. God was unyielding because this had nothing to do with *my* wishes nor my perceptions of my talents. "Go where I send you for *my* sake." So, fearfully, I went.

I don't remember a word I said, but the words came. I was faithful and opened my mouth, and God told the story. He had not filled me with knowledge even one moment before I began. But he was there with me precisely as I started.

God does not call us because we have great gifts, talents, or wisdom. He doesn't need perfection. He only asks for willingness—willingness to be used. And when we "show up," he can be counted on to enable us to fulfill the task. His enabling is what we lean on, not our own. In fact our own efforts can be guaranteed to get in the way.

God will not send me—or you—where he cannot use us. The trouble, generally, lies in convincing us to go.

One speech led to many others, to radio and television interviews. I learned that lengthy interviews and publicized media exposures weren't necessary for success—my briefest interviews often elicited the greatest responses. God's way goes counter to human expectation. He will use even ten minutes, with unmatchable power, if we offer it to him. It doesn't take long hours or polished phrases to be a 1980s disciple. It doesn't demand a long career in the mission field or the ministry. One need only have a street, a home, a store—and be faithful.

Often the letters written to me will speak longingly of a desire for a new perspective, or taking up some adventurous challenge or mission for Christ. Women tell me, "I wish I might be called, like you, to travel and spread the Christian message." Or, "I'd love to counsel many needy souls."

But travel and great numbers of people have nothing whatever to do with serving Christ. That's our mistaken notion, and that's precisely why we are often such careless servants of his, where it counts the most.

The formula for finding your own, primary mission is here:

Put down this book.

Walk outside your house, trailer, or apartment.
Look in through a window.
Now you see where Christ has sent you. Serving
starts right where you are. If you understand that your
mission to the faces at your table, no matter how few,
ranks in importance with the mission of a great evange-
list to crowds of thousands, then you have begun to
understand Love. A life of service is to carry out that
meaning.

God tells me: "When you would do what I may ask
with no one noticing, then you are mine. Don't love for
the sake of publicity or notoriety or success or filled
churches. Love because I say to love. Unless fame
comes as a by-product it will be a god, so continually
put your achievements on my altar. Only when you can
leave them there is it safe to have them. I am God."

All of us are disciples. Single or married, alone or
together. All called.

3
WITH
OTHER
EYES

It is the spirit in a man,
the breath of the Almighty,
that makes him understand.
Job 32:8

NAVAL CAPTAINS HAVE PROBABLY PROCEEDED into battle with less thought than I have sometimes given my clothes when preparing for a trip. Somehow, at that moment of packing, it seems very important to be bringing what's "right."

Will I need a suit more than a sweater? But then, I'm always cold. Is there room for a frivolous evening dress, *just in case?* Should I squeeze in an extra pair of shoes? Choice after choice, many made in light of the real limitations of weight and space. Deciding which things are necessities and which are mere fun and frills requires time, planning, and care.

But at no closet should we stand more critically than before the one that holds the belongings we'll carry on life's inner journey, for there are hung the attitudes, ideas, and beliefs that we continually wear. In the material world these attitudes may seem inconsequential, but in terms of a spiritual journey, many of these ideas and beliefs cost us a lot to bring along. They weigh us down. They hold us back.

For me, one such subtle but costly attitude is a too often critical heart which judges and measures all others by their likeness in thought, word, and deed to myself. Think like me, the voice whispers, and then you're okay. Agree with me, act like me, and then I'll approve.

One afternoon at lunch Beth and I argued round and round about a dinky, cardboard Lifesaver case which she wanted to keep, and which I felt should be thrown away. I'm not a saver, and the inside of me told me to clear away all "useless clutter." "Let's face it," I reasoned with Beth in perfect parental tones, "you can't keep every cardboard wrapper you love." Beth sighed.

Finally she suggested, "Well, can I at least throw the case away in my own wastebasket upstairs?" With a shrug I agreed, considering the issue dealt with.

Later that week I reluctantly tackled the challenge of cleaning Beth's room. The electric broom was pushing easily across the floor when suddenly there was a snap followed by a sick *Whirrrrrr.* The broom nozzle was choking on some object caught beneath Beth's bureau. I bent over and tugged at edges of colored paper, and there in my hand was the treasured, much-discussed cardboard Lifesaver case.

I stared at it for a long while. I had spent all morning thinking and writing about the beautiful differences in people, for a speech I was to deliver that weekend. I had planned to advise listeners to relax their strangle hold on others, their attempt to bring all things in line with *their* values, their perceptions, their personal codes. I wanted to show how easy it is to sit and smugly disapprove of mothers who raise their children differently, teen-age friends whose dress or values do not conform to ours, friends who have unique tastes in art or music, peers who have their own goals, churches which have their own distinctives. Our criticisms are endless, limited only by our own inventiveness.

But when do we ever stop to thank God *for* the differences? True beauty is seen when millions upon millions of unique faces are free to be themselves, when private judgment refuses to demand total conformity.

Intellectually most of us would agree about this. But actually, day to day, where it counts, we are guilty, all of us, of being effective dimmers of others' lights. And there I stood in Beth's bedroom, self-convicted, a repeat offender.

It happens so easily, our taking the treasures of others, parts of their very selves, and discarding them. A husband's love for fishing which a wife doesn't share. A wife's need to chat with friends all afternoon, which may seem to a husband a waste of time. A child's decision to be something that his parents never dreamed that their child would be. A person's right to worship God differently. A loved one's right to make a mistake. A friend's prerogative to make decisions about the future in his own right time. A widow's need to grieve in her own way.

It's frightening how easily we will wound when the particular ideas *we* have for life feel threatened. Sometimes, too often, I wound another's spirit by my own harsh expectations, by my lack of approval, by withholding encouragement, by severe criticism and condemnation, by coldly denying love, by my unwillingness to share the joy in another's life when that happiness has not resulted from my actions.

Tough issues. Crucial issues which show themselves in trivial ways, in corners or under furniture. And so I held Beth's cardboard case in my hand for a long while; then I reached down beneath her bureau and shoved the tiny box in against the wall.

No, you can't ultimately keep every little cardboard box in the world. Yes, Beth *will* eventually have to face the fact that life is full of compromise and some wishes can't be met. But that wasn't the story.

I suppose the essence of this is tolerance and respect,

and yet it's more. Love is always more. It's a warning against looking at the outside of things, or people, for complete answers. They won't be there. How caught up we become in staring at differences, resenting them, fearing them.

The point is that underneath *all* appearances, no matter how disguised, lives another person no less valuable than you. Christianity begins there. And until we can look in any face and be convinced, "No less than me," then it hasn't begun in our lives.

In the end, the security of sameness is false. The fullness of life begins when we meet differences with love.

I think about differences and the faces of people all the time.

I remember one morning in July during one of my stays at a small rented cottage on the Connecticut shore. Beth delighted in all the days of sun, and I did too. But my best times were early, before dawn, when I would walk along the shoreline, alone with the dark grey sea. At that hour the beach is always quiet. The lusty disco beats which blare all afternoon from radios lugged by the young are silent early in the morning. No melodies, no words interrupt dawn's reign. The only voice is the lapping ocean, waking.

That particular morning it was chilly, and I'd pulled on my worn blue sweater as protection against the cool, offshore breeze. Though the just-risen sun, red and full, had found the jagged rocks at a distant point to my left, and warmly covered them, its light had not yet discovered me. A foot or so from the water's edge I crouched down on the sand and looked far up along the beach. And I waited.

Gradually other daybreak lovers began to pass by. Some looked at me, smiling, wondering, perhaps, why I sat each dawn with my note pad, and what I wrote; they were unaware that I was writing about them.

That day a couple were the first to walk by, fingers tenderly brushing, shyly in love. Their faces reflected the waking light and I envied their harmony. A family jogged past, some members sweaty and red-faced, but all determined. Doggedly they pursued the long reaches of the shore. Then two young boys trudged noisily by, Huck Finns, water sloshing in the pails where they hoped to capture treasures at the water's edge. Friends passed, deep in conversation. Others walked singly, their thoughts silent beneath the sky's brightening blue. One woman passed me crying. And then a man colored with anger. In effect, he was crying, too.

Then my favorites: crusty old women, their portly shapes wrapped without thought of fashion in tight-fitting pants and baggy sweatshirts, plodding purposefully along behind slim silver metal detectors, offering hours of the morning for maybe two pennies.

It is a present, this hour and these people. It is the morning and the world presenting itself to me. It is all the players acting out the drama of their individual lives. There are no bit parts. Each face assumes a special role.

And life isn't a crowd. It is a one-by-one affair. We

are called to it one by one and we respond in the same way.

David's Psalm 139 is a stirring testimony to our separate lives and how highly they are regarded by God—how much they matter. He says, "Lord, thou art intimately acquainted with all my ways... Thou didst form my inward parts; thou didst weave me in my mother's womb... I am fearfully and wonderfully made. My frame was not hidden from thee when I was being made in secret and intricately wrought in the depths of the earth. Thine eyes saw my unformed substance; in thy book were written every one of the days that were ordained for me." If this applies to me, then it applies to you. And every man and woman. This is the miracle of being personally planned and wanted and loved by God.

Jesus showed us even more about how we are separately cared for. "Indeed, the very hairs of your head are all numbered," he said in Luke 12:7.

I think that in the end we'll find that achieving similarities in our journeys was not God's intention at all. There were meant to be endlessly diverse expressions of beauty. That's what the faces I see tell me. And we must learn in our living together to honor differences.

I am also addicted to city streets, and sometimes I go to New York City for a day, or two, and just walk and watch. None of us should die without recognizing the beauty of humanity. Any kind of ritual or enforced segregation is not only sinful, but a profound misunderstanding of what humanity, and life, are all about. The Prado or the Met or the Louvre may leave us awestruck. Incomparable art hangs on their walls. But there is equal magnificence in one hundred lives drawn from any city block precisely because each is so different.

When I walk in hard places I see drunks in city gutters with no hope. Or dear, frail bag ladies with unruly hair, dirty kerchiefs and no place to go. There are the successful young executives who aren't really happy, for all of their brilliant achievements, and high-fashion models and film stars who smile to cover the emptiness of fame and wealth. I see families with sacks of fresh produce, struggling and loving day by day, wondering if they'll make it, wondering if they'll find jobs. I pass drug-crazed eyes whose owners have entered realms which are hardly human—hells on earth. I see minorities who live what it means to be hated, daily, because of a difference in their skin or their speech or their education.

And even this view is only a fragment of the whole. In Third World countries are the beggars and illiterates and primitives and those who never have had and never *will* have a decent chance. In Iron Curtain countries are searching faces who will never know an hour without the threat of persecution, who have to *guess* at how freedom might feel. In India and Uganda and Brazil are children who will spend every day of their lives hungry. Every single day.

And I think that the most culpable faces in God's sight are our own—well-scrubbed, fed, privileged, and too often indifferent.

No, I am not naive enough to think that one man or one woman can change India. Nor did you personally create that or any other atrocity. Yes, if you sold your belongings and gave all that you have, people would still be hungry and homeless. And no, I don't doubt that in spite of a lifetime of effort on your part, some innocent children would still be brutally abused, and molested, and murdered in spirit. I don't doubt any of it. And neither does God. But those impossible tasks are not what he is calling you or me to do.

He is not asking that individual men or women achieve accomplishments of immediate global significance.

He asks that we struggle to see the world with other eyes. Eyes more like his own. He asks that we care about other human beings, those with whom we live and interact every day. That we weep with those who weep. Share our goods with the less fortunate. Clothe the naked. Accept those whose thoughts and values do not mimic our own. Forgive.

We are called to reflect the light of love and to be that light in a mocking world. And we are all of us accountable to that love.

Love is hard. It is threatening to think that our lives might be jarred, our money requested, our time demanded, our compassion tested, and our love exposed for what it really is, and for how far it really goes.

But if we re-read the New Testament and if Christ is fully heard, it becomes clear that today's church, claiming to live on in his name, too often has little resemblance to the church which he established.

He sat down and ate with sinners. The tax collectors were his friends. All were drawn to his healing compassion, his unconditional love. And he told us to go on in like manner. How do we measure up?

We miss the mark when all church members do not feel themselves to be living parts of God's own team. For in this world *we* are the gospel. We miss the mark when anyone feels that no one cares. We miss the mark when we persecute others for differences, right in our own midst. We miss the mark whenever the widowed and fatherless are not tended and cared for by many hands. We miss the mark when those who do not conform to society's rigid mores are not genuinely welcomed. We miss the mark when we are not all willing to share our goods and talents when someone is in need. We miss the mark when we think that the church ends in a building or structure or service on Sundays. We miss the mark when the gospel doesn't make of us lovers of our neighborhoods and streets. We miss the mark when we feel no unity with the world crying in need, when we convince ourselves that we are not the brother or sister of every prisoner, murderer, addict, homosexual, or deranged soul.

Do we sometimes sit inside, complacently singing hymns when God needs us outside doing his work? Disciples. Real disciples called by Jesus today. That is the deep meaning of the body of Christ. His hands are not separate from ours.

Several weeks ago my prayer group discussed this very issue. We were talking about the churches in New York City which the mayor had asked to provide shelter for the homeless at a particular holiday time. The plan hadn't worked and someone in the group explained that almost all of those city churches had refused to help. It was simply too impractical, they said, in terms of financial realities. Hundreds of dollars might have to be spent to turn on needed electricity, heat, etc., and even then, only one or two needy people might show.

Only two people in need might have come, but what if one had been Christ?

"Lord, when did we see you hungry, or thirsty, or a stranger, or naked, or sick, or in prison, and did not take care of you? Then he will answer them saying, Truly I say to you, to the extent that you did not do it to one of the least of these, you did not do it to me."³

I must take personally Jesus' challenge to "come, follow me," to set my mind on "God's interests, not man's." Leading a good and decent life is not enough, for "he who is not with me is against me."

Several winters ago a raging night fire totally destroyed a church in a town several miles from my home and the incident was widely viewed as a great tragedy.

Privately I thought that the parish was lucky. Reports were that members of the congregation had huddled together outside the burning walls and wept. And then they joined hands. They sang Christmas carols from borrowed song sheets in the still of that cold, cold December night. And they understood Bethlehem.

Social cliques and warring committees were forgotten for that night. All rejoiced in life and the lack of any injuries. No one gave thought to how they were attired or whether or not their voice was pleasing. They wept because they were clothed at all, and able to sing.

On the fringes of their gathering others began to join

in. Arms reached out to welcome nonmembers. No one belonged any more or less than anyone else. No one criticized. No one felt afraid to approach the others and ask to be included. No one was ashamed to cry.

That night all were worthy.

Oddly it is often our poverty, and that alone, which can reveal to us our wealth. Mercy is what the message of Jesus was all about.

4
UNLIKELY
MESSENGER

You do not know the path
of the wind ... even so,
you do not know the works
of the Lord, who makes all.
Ecclesiastes 11:5

WHEN WE WERE KIDS my sisters and I were always referred to as "the twins and Paula." They were one entity, and I was someone else, apart. Consequently my vivid imagination began creating my own companions, and I learned this art of fantasy thoroughly. Often I would play in my room with paper dolls, creating lives for each of them hour after hour. Part of the charm, I suppose, was having such complete control of my imaginary world. In dreams life can always fulfill your dearest wish.

My strongest dream was to have my own real pal. It was, of course, too late for me to hope to be a twin. And yet I imagined someone who would be that close, who would love me, especially.

And then my brother Peter arrived. How triumphant I felt! A partner at last!

I watched Peter daily, impatient at my mother's side, eager for this round, wholesome newborn to grow. It was as if I were calling to him, "Hurry up, won't you? Can't you see how long I've been waiting? It took you all this time to get here. Now catch up!"

As if to satisfy my impatience he learned to roll over quickly. He picked up other things fast, too. He was so eager and wore a forever smile. And he reached into me and tapped deep springs of love. I knew he loved me too.

I was a clown. And since my silly antics made Peter laugh, I would play with him for hours. He bounced in a yellow johnny jump-up while I invented countless games. I took him out and watched him roll. I crept into his crib and slept beside him. I strung him with rosary

beads, like jewels, and played "church." For months
the dimensions of my world were simple and good. I
had longed for and received the answer to a very special
dream. I delighted in this brother and in this world of
which I was in control. I trusted all the safe boundaries
of my life. There was no harm anywhere that I could
see.

A little child unfurls slowly
To a magic world, filled with wonders.
His life a season of splendor
Replete with angels of love and benevolent giants.
—Charles Doss.[4]

But I didn't know everything. I didn't know that
within deep joy, within its essence, is also the possibility of deep sorrow. And only fools, those who fool
themselves, think they can open their arms to embrace
one without the other. They cannot be separated; to live
safe, protected, controlled lives is to run as far from joy,
and just as fast, as we do from tears. "When we kill the
intolerable, we also kill what's gentle and good."   In
January of 1951 Peter had a terrible cold. All children
have their share of viruses and colds, so nothing
seemed amiss in that; illness is a fact of life. I played by
myself again for a week that winter, waiting for Peter's
fever to leave and everything to be fine. But the days
multiplied and everything was *not* fine.

The doctor came, checked, and reassured with words.
But Peter's symptoms denied all the physician's efforts
to calm us. My eyes took in scenes which were too
frightening to accept: convulsions, my parents' alarm,
hospitals, new doctors. Day was not smoothly following

day. Something *was* amiss. Peter was so sick. They rushed him to the hospital.

My father sat us down together, the twins and me, and told us carefully that Peter was a very sick boy. He had spinal meningitis and he would never, ever be well again. The sickness had stolen his speech, perhaps his sight, his limbs, his brain. The robbery was complete except that the raw stuff of living, his breath, would keep him alive. (Was that life, or was it death? I didn't know.)

I listened to each one of my father's statements. I think I needed him to pick me up and hold me, but he was swimming in his own pain. So I went by myself to my room. In a few minutes I had begun to grow up. I knew the two inseparable sides of joy, and part of me could never be small and innocent again.

For long days I waited for Peter. I never dreamed it would be so bad when he returned home from the hospital. I could only imagine him laughing or screaming —the extremes. But it was to be neither. Even though he returned to our house with the same rooms, the same people, he was in the grip of a different reality. Peter was now living in a quiet cocoon.

He would never run. It would be difficult for him to move at all. He would never call my name or be able to tell us when he felt pain. He might or might not hear the things I would tell him. Whether he did or not he would just be still. It was as if someone had said, "Here, keep life. But all your other gifts have been recalled."

I could not understand.

Wherever Peter sat, surrounded by great pillows, we

would tuck a small toy next to him. Sometimes his fingers closed around a rattle and he shook it, with a small spasm, into the air. And then it would drop on to the cluster of teddy bears, lambs, and bunnies which surrounded him. Sometimes he would kick and punch at them, seemingly in delight.

Without support his head would fall to one side, and without my mother's care he was completely helpless. But even so he always smiled. And laughed. He didn't seem to know that he shouldn't have wanted to. Does a lot of our conscious sadness come from there, from knowing our circumstances and believing that they have been assigned a "sad" label? Is the sadness in the circumstances or in the believing?

In the fall we propped Peter up in his grey carriage and wheeled him around. He wore a red corduroy cap and he smiled into the breezes. As the leaves turned color I told him how and why, and described for him what he couldn't see. Later, when there was snow, I sneaked some in for him to feel. I tried to break life down into small pieces so that we could go over it together.

By the time he was four years old he was growing much too heavy for my mother to carry around all the time, so when summertime arrived my father built a tall white "cage" on wheels. Then we could raise the door, lay Peter inside and push him around for a ride in the warm air. We called it Peter's "coop." Since I was small enough to fit inside too, I often rode with him, content as my father pushed us about. Back and forth we journeyed, crossing a square of blacktop in our backyard like voyagers on a concrete sea. Best friends, we sailed a thousand crossings.

As Peter and the details of his care grew, so did the order of our household. Everyone's schedule had to adjust to Peter's rigorous needs. And surely, more than once, my parents felt that their strength had met the end of human endurance. Battles with bitterness and exhaustion must have been waged. Battles with despair. Each meal meant a feeding, a vomiting, and a patient refeeding. The laundering of diapers and soiled clothing was continuous, and the tension of convulsions often filled the night. And there was often a cry from Peter for which there was no comfort—a haunting cry. I hold a picture of my father, weary beyond hope, coming home from work to walk miles of love, back and forth through the rooms, carrying his crying boy on his shoulder. I think nothing in his life will ever erase those miles.

Yet how gratefully I credit my parents that love was still left over to fill three other young lives with so much that was good. There were no family vacations, no trips together to view the wonders promoted by the media, no sports events played with parents cheering at our sides. But we were given diversity and richness in other ways.

Chief among our pleasures was the magic of music, my father's innate sense of harmony and song seeming to flood each of us in turn. We three sisters learned the harmonies my father set to popular tunes and filled many evenings and car rides with our own singing. Or we would sit by the hour listening to my father's piano playing, learning decades of lyrics to familiar tunes. The exceptional opportunity of the highly advantaged is not the only possible encouragement to creative expression. What is there to be born can be born anywhere, if love awakens it.

And so my own inclination toward drama led to numerous kitchen productions, complete with costumes, melodramatic plots and, I'm sure, the most amateur acting to be found. But we laughed in spite of pain. With it. Because of it. And in being laughed with, and loved, we all felt the greatest strength that can be given.

During these years, as I stayed by Peter's side for long hours, a new feeling began to grow within me. I started to feel that my life, somehow, bore a responsibility for his. If he had lost his capacity for sensation and rationality then I wanted to redouble mine. I wanted to see for his eyes, feel for his heart, think for his mind, live all of my life more deeply because he who was such a part of me would never consciously experience his life at all.

Seeking such intensity, I soon began to find it. I felt myself becoming strongly affected by the natural world, loving both its subtleties and its extremes: gentle twilights and fierce, baking suns; delicate rains and furious hurricanes. I was drawn again and again to the sea, its bay visible from my window. I loved the passion of racing whitecaps, and grew up bracing my swimsuited body against waves twice my height. The sea was authentic. Whether gentle, insistent with undertow, or restless with rolling swells, it honestly showed me what it was, its truth calming me, easing, in a way, the grief I felt for my brother's limited life.

I began to realize that life offers, without explanation, both of what Sheldon Vanauken calls "incredible joy and intolerable pain." *Offers.* And I decided then, early on, to accept the full scope of life, with all its risks. And Peter was responsible for that choice as much as I.

Months passed and the effects of meningitis continued to rage through Peter's body. In spite of his disease he grew—longer, heavier, more burdensome to carry. His hair was black and fine, his eyes a midnight brown soberly looking out beneath thick, long lashes. He ought to have been swinging plastic baseball bats and driving three older sisters crazy; instead he lay silently, totally dependent upon someone's care.

When I was nine years old, and Peter five, there began to be evenings of low conversations between my parents, relatives, and close friends. My parents seemed old, and pain was written in their features. I wasn't included in their discussions and I didn't know what was going on, but I could sense an aura of heartache and could feel their growing despair.

One day suitcases appeared at the back door, and we were all sat down for a family discussion. We were told that Peter had grown beyond my mother's physical strength. Bigger, stronger helpers were needed to lift and carry him, to care for him. There were no longer resources in our home for his protection and care. And with these words was introduced a stinging new reality: Peter was being taken to a carefully selected state school. That next day he left.

I was told that state regulations would prevent me from visiting him until I was sixteen years old, and that was seven years away. Love, for the first time, had been packed up and moved away. Inside I screamed without any words.

Now every Sunday the family which had known no travel had a regular outing. We followed beautiful, green, tree-lined backroads through small New England towns to the school where Peter now lived. I memorized the route by the color of the houses and the positions of the trees. How familiar that route became! My sisters and I would sit in the back seat of the car, reading, playing, fighting, while my parents went inside to hold their child. They must have needed to cry— or rage. But no one ever did so in front of me. They just bore the separation and kept on.

Sometimes as I sat in the car, idly watching people on the grounds, I thought of what I believed to be true but couldn't dare tell anyone: that if Peter could see me, could know that I hadn't left him, then miraculously he would be well. I believed that for a long time.

My years between nine and sixteen were rich with experiences, questions, and dreams. I was never to find one special companion to replace Peter, and I carried his memory into my growing years. My life was filled with afternoon band rehearsals, cheer-leading practices, and a wide assortment of clubs. And I, born impatient, had a driver's permit signed, sealed, and waiting for the morning I turned sixteen. Eventually (but with great reluctance) my father succumbed to my persistent pleas that he take me to practice drive. We did an angry internship in Sunday parking lots and deserted roads. Someone was always ready to kill someone when we returned home. But in spite of hysterics I was one day ready to test my skills on real, driveable roads. And I knew just which ones and where I wanted to go. And so my father and I set out to see Peter. I was facing two adventures in one longed-for moment.

The drive, at least from my perspective, was not so bad. My father swore some and looked grim, but none of the trees or shoulders toward which I'd swerved had *actually.* been hit. So all was well in my eyes. I little dreamed that my destination, and not the getting there, would be the trial.

In my heart, as my father and I walked down the grey corridor to Peter's room, was the picture I had held for seven years of a chubby, beautiful, dark-haired boy who smiled in response to gentle sounds and filled me with the marvel of his presence. I recalled my childish beliefs of a miraculous cure. Even short of that, I still felt that life was righting itself in our reuniting. I walked, almost ran, to Peter's bed in my joy.

But a hard reality met me. He was Peter, and yet he was not, he was so drastically changed. He lay long and thin—much, much thinner than I had ever imagined. Beautiful lashes still framed the deepest brown eyes, but his once full cheeks were now taut and sunken. I could not find the smile that I remembered. Seven years had taken their toll. Peter lay with an absent stare. It was as if the price of his life had been too great.

I fought rising tears and nausea simultaneously, not knowing which heaving would be greater. I wanted to run from the building into the surrounding, protective woods. I just wanted to go. And all that kept me there was the bond once so tightly formed with him, my counterpart.

I sat with effort beside the bed's iron rail and softly told him, "Peter, it's me." When I touched him, he stirred slightly and I called again, "Peter." I believed he heard me and understood. But I will never know. And there was no miracle.

In September of 1965 I started college. Inwardly I was full of fears, dreading the separation from my family. Outwardly I was full of confidence and kept repeating, "I can't wait to leave this place!" I suppose I couldn't have left if I'd handled it any other way.

I never told anyone, but one of the factors in my choice of a college was that the one I had selected lay only six miles from that other school where my brother still barely existed. Being so close was no real advantage since I had no car to get me there. But the awareness of my proximity helped me to feel good. Peter and I were close together once again.

For me college was an island of adjustments. It was an introduction to life's lesson, "You're on your own." And I fought my way through many quandaries in the initial months, acclimating myself to the wonder and responsibility of having no one tell me what to do. Gradually I became comfortable with a close group of friends and I settled into the serious business of passing my courses.

One evening, just two days past the celebration of my eighteenth birthday I sat struggling over calculus equations. The work was hard and required every glimmer of brain-power I could summon. Then a phone call interrupted me. I was still mentally figuring calculus when I heard my father's voice. He took care with his words, but even so they were a knife, and they cut and wounded as his voice moved through the ear piece. "Peter has gone," he said. "Early this morning. It's all over."

I didn't cry. I went to my typewriter and pounded out three pages of love, confusion, and memories. I packed my bags. And when a neighbor from home arrived, I rode quietly home, watching the stars. It was very black, I remember, and when I came to my house everyone was calm. I mimicked their control.

The funeral was a Mass of the Angels, and Peter's casket was white. It was rolled softly down the long church aisle, its wheels singing over the thin carpet. There were flowers and incense, and something burned and choked my throat. I couldn't look at anyone. But when I saw my father's face, I wanted to cry. I wanted to cry hard, but I wouldn't let it begin.

Relatives and friends returned to our home and everyone talked in small clusters. "It was a blessing."

"Now it's over."

"It's been going on so long."

There was coffee and punch and cake. But no one said to me, "Do you need to cry?" or "I know how you loved him so." They talked about other things late into the evening. And eventually I went to my bedroom and felt the sturdy, warm, maple branches I could reach from my window, and stared into the black night.

In the middle of that night I was very sick. The following day, my body heaved continuously and violently and the illness would not stop. The next night was the famous blackout of 1965, but I was too ill to care.

There was a blackout inside me as well.

For a week I tried each morning to return to school, but I couldn't recover. For weeks more a gnawing nausea never left me. I learned to go on, but it was months before the sick feeling finally went away.

Peter had died in cold November. And one day the following spring I walked into the woods surrounding my campus and sat on a stone and wept. I cried for life and death and absence and for all that he'd meant to me. No one had known then. No one would ever know. And after a long while I whispered, "Good-bye."

Many, many miles later into my life I started trying to piece together the "why" behind my brother's life. He was rare, he was beautiful, he was different. Anyone who's loved someone who's brain-damaged or retarded will instantly know. Regardless of who he was outside, inside he was a well of love. And, an even greater treasure, he allowed himself to be fully loved by another.

Peter never spoke, yet I heard two things. First, that no moment and no part of creation is without meaning, be it perfect or imperfect. And so we make a terrible error when we make a god of perfection, and outward beauty and form. God's face is not to be found reflected only in excellence, as we'd like to believe. It glints from every corner and movement, for all life is his. Every day God surprises us without our expecting him.

So lest our expectations limit and deceive us, we'd do well to begin believing that any part of creation, at any time, may speak his name to our particular heart. Then all becomes valuable, and nothing is purely regret or loss or insignificance.

Thus while Peter never spoke or played, still he

vitally interacted with me and his presence greatly shaped who I was to become. In one sense everything about him was damaged, imperfect. But as God loved and used him that was no longer so.

Second, Peter taught me about possession. Or maybe it was about letting go. Through illness he had left his mental faculties and motor abilities behind him. He left physically, geographically, when he was taken from our lives to the state school. And then he left through death. But it all said this to me: since there are no parts of ourselves, or our lives, that we can safely own, then every effort toward possession and its seeming security inches us toward counterfeit hopes and false reality— reality in which we race after shadows.

What matters is not owning life (which is impossible), but sanctifying it with love while we have it. Recognizing it as the fleeting, precious gift it is. And recognizing ourselves as co-celebrants in what it means to be alive. "I am alive for another day. I think of those who aren't."[5]

Is it tragedy to have full life within you and not care? To not use it? To create distance and division? To lie to yourself? To deny the person you are able to be?

And if you *do* struggle to become everything you might be, does that make a difference in the world? Do any of our stories matter? In the end I know my days with Peter were all they needed to be. They could not have been more. But does the love or lack of love or indifference to love in your life or mine change nothing? Or everything?

I think the latter.

5
PIECES
OF
GOD

Nothing we do is unimportant.
Even our thoughts generate
a force which affects the universe.
J. Bronowski

"I'M 34 YEARS OLD, AND SINCE I WAS 24 I have been living in a 'twilight zone,' neither alive nor dead. I believe through reading your book that God is showing me that He did not fail you, and if I trust Him, He will not fail me. But I will only trust Him if I can understand *why* this has happened and *why* I am neither healed nor allowed to die."

The letter containing these words was my introduction to a young man whose agonized world was to touch my own in a powerful, life-changing way. I had no hint of that at the start (I guess that's usually the way) but I still shudder when I remember how close I came to not knowing Ken Harper at all.

Such "chances" always remind me of the C. S. Lewis tale of Narnia in which Aslan, the beloved lion, has told young Lucy which path she is to follow. But when Lucy is unable to convince her other companions that this is the path they are meant to take (Aslan's instructions do not make "human" sense), she gives in to the others and goes the way they have chosen.

That wrongly chosen path looked like the easiest way to reach their destination. But even as they round the first bend it proves to be filled with unimagined difficulties. As every step becomes harder their happy journey becomes increasingly arduous, and they are often close to despair.

When the destination is finally reached, everyone rejoices, and it is in the midst of this celebration that Lucy spies Aslan and meets him for the second time.

She deeply regrets not having followed his instruction, and begs him to tell her what *his* path would have been like. Was it in fact easier, even though at first glance it didn't seem to be? Was it better, she wants to know?

Aslan regards her tenderly. She is very dear. But she must know the truth: No one is ever given to know what *might have been*.

It is painfully true that I initially fought knowing Ken Harper. I've wondered if my reaction to his first letter might have been different had it arrived alone. But it didn't. Ken showed up first in the flood of mail generated by the December, 1980 *Reader's Digest* condensation of my book, *Song For Sarah*. Grocery bags full of letters lined my kitchen floor, and the task of answering each note seemed so overwhelming that I felt close to tears every time I walked past them.

I think I had worked my way through two full bags when I wearily reached Ken's letter. My sister Anne, who was helping me to sort and stamp, had put his letter aside in a pile marked "special."

To start with, Ken's "note" was eight pages long, with both sides of each page filled with his heavy, angular, hard-to-decipher script.

In the letter he outlined for me his particular physical disabilities and suffering, which were great. And then he begged for my help. He had countless questions about God, life, and suffering and he needed to ask me all of them. He was so sure I was the one to ask.

I was equally sure I was not! My eyes were already red-rimmed from weeks of mail, travel, and the care of a four-year-old child. I knew one thing for sure: I didn't have time for such lengthy correspondence. I could barely squeeze time to send my mother periodic postcards to report that Beth and I were alive. And besides *all* of that, I wasn't sure I had the answers to his kinds of questions.

So I wrote back to Ken and suggested that he seek some counseling right in his own city, or that he find a minister with whom he could more easily thrash out all of his questions and ideas. And when the envelope with my reply was sealed, I mentally dismissed the whole issue.

But for the following three months Ken never stopped writing to me. He'd try first one approach, then another. And he insisted over and over that it was *me* that he needed to talk with. In every lengthy letter he asked me to please reconsider.

And I knew for sure that I didn't want to do it; I didn't have the time; I wasn't qualified; his problems were far too serious; period.

While he was young, tests performed on Ken had revealed that the drainage passage from his brain had slowly closed, causing fluid to accumulate. A hundred years ago there would have been little hope for such a child. However, medical practice in 1954 allowed the doctors to drain the excess fluid from seven-year-old Ken's brain and give him some expectation of normal life.

For the next few years Ken's functioning seemed to be completely normal. However, in 1960 some hearing loss was first measured and gradually Ken developed a condition known as tinnitus—a persistent, maddening ringing in the ears which was to overshadow and eventually dominate the rest of his life.

Its effects began mildly, but steadily accelerated. At the time of his letters to me he had been suffering without relief for ten years. The constant noise left him virtually deaf. And tormented.

Ken and his parents had visited every doctor and clinic which offered any hope of a solution, or of even some small relief. He tried the medicines and masking devices which are helpful to some who suffer in this manner. But for Ken those attempts were not successful, and so he lived in an inner prison, wondering why the God of love whom he'd been raised to worship could remain so distant and silent.

He was calling out to God. He'd repeatedly read the Bible from cover to cover. He memorized Scripture passages about faith, and read over and over the Bible accounts of those who had been healed.

And he prayed to be healed. He believed with all his heart that he would be. But he wasn't. Finally he begged only for relief, if not healing. But there was still no change.

Now he was writing to me saying, "Answer my questions. Listen to my arguments. Withstand my anger. Argue back at me. Please. Show me, in my pain, how to find the God you know."

The frequency of Ken's letters mounted, and although I was wrestling with his plight in my heart, I just didn't know how to help. I tucked the letters into my desk drawer but it couldn't contain them. Emotionally I was carrying them. They were always with me.

Until one day, without any grand forethought, I just sat down and wrote "Okay." My assent was not out of kindness, not yet out of love It had simply become harder to deny this impossible task than to face it. I wondered casually if it was God, or me, or God in me, who wouldn't let me rest until I'd finally agreed to respond.

My every hesitation and fear was soon realized as Ken began to write back with pages and pages of questions which I was ill-qualified to answer. As I responded from my heart, as best I could, Ken, with his superior intelligence, took all of my beliefs apart, inch by inch. Soon I was spending hours writing eight- to ten-page letters, only to reach stalemate after stalemate.

And yet imperceptibly a strong friendship began to grow. If Ken's reply to one of my letters was too long in coming, I began to worry that he was sicker, or that the pain had finally defeated his spirit. Sometimes my own traveling caused my responses to be delayed, and then a worried telegram would arrive from Ken, or a phone call, placed by his father or brother on Ken's behalf. Our spirits had become strangely intertwined.

Since Ken's suffering was never far from me, I began to internalize and agonize over his own questions to God. Why, if you are love, does life contain such pain? How, God, can you allow a human being to suffer so without help? Why are some people healed and others not? What is there about you that we fail to understand? Please teach me, God!

During our long letters of 1981 I could say only one thing that seemed to earn no rebuttal from Ken. I knew that for any man to know and love God fully, he must have "no other strange gods" before him—the first commandment. But strange gods, in acceptable clothing, are hard to uncover. Careers. Independence. Children.

Spouses. Money. Dreams. An insistent demand for answers to all our *whys.* Pride.

None of these listed items is wrong in and of itself. Each is a rich part of life. It is in their priority, their coming first—that only—that they become strange gods. Even human love—yes, especially love—deceives us when it takes over God's position in our life's rightful order.

The simple truth is that whatever you *have* to have, whatever you trust the most, becomes your god.

Ken's honesty touched me deeply. He would admit, "After all that I have been through, how hard it is, sometimes, to believe that God is, or that he cares. I feel like a joke has been perpetrated on me. I feel like God was leading me, had told me to wait for further directions and then left (abandoned) me. I've been left. God's refusal to take away my pain... brings out the anger in me. Do I believe he knows best? My life is such a shambles, I wonder. If only I could have even a piece of what you have—your faith, your sight of God."

When I tried to respond to Ken I felt, always, that my position was untenable. What did I know? Everything I said was voiced from a position of relative health and plenty. How much easier it was for me. If I were Ken, I wondered if my outrage and self-pity might not have been worse. I wondered especially if I'd even have searched for God. I had an idea I might have let pain, fear, and despair take full control.

In January of 1982 Ken boldly wrote that he had a dream: He wanted to meet me in person. He wrote that he imaged it daily, that in his mind he saw it happening. He had decided that the only likely spot would be St.

Louis or Kansas City, both near to his Kansas home. I
would come to speak and then his folks would bring
him to see me.

He wrote continually of that dream. He prayed for it,
in spite of his anger with God, and I ached every time
he mentioned it. I had never been to Missouri or Kansas
to speak, and I couldn't foresee it happening. The worst
of it was to think of Ken praying another unlikely-to-be-
answered prayer.

Three weeks later my phone rang in the early morning. It was one of those moments when you are just
leaving the house and you pause, debating whether or
not to delay yourself by running back to the phone. It is
characteristic of me to keep on going. But that day I
went back for the phone.

The television talk show, "Something Beautiful,"
hosted by Jane Park, was calling from Kansas City to see
if Beth and I could possibly fly out in three weeks to
tape a show. I talked my way through all the details and
arrangements as if in a vacuum. When I hung up I was
still staring at my wall.

Among the things in life I didn't know were why Ken
suffered so and why he couldn't find God. I didn't
know why faith came so hard to him. I didn't know
why he lived when he wished to die. But I *did* know that
we were about to meet. I knew that he had prayed for it
to be so and that this was one prayer about to be
answered.

I wrote to him immediately, my urgent errand forgotten, and my feet several inches off the pavement as I
ran to post the letter. Joy flies, or seems to.

Three weeks passed quickly, and on the February day

of the taping it was seventy degrees and spring-like in Kansas City. Our winter coats and wool clothing made us seem like unprepared travelers in a strange land.

Since my in-laws lived in Missouri, they were joining us for the morning. When we finished taping they would drive me to Ken's brother's home where I would meet him. Beth could meet Ken for a few minutes, too, then spend the afternoon with her grandparents.

If it's possible to be terrified and excited at the same time, I was. I wanted to do this. I cared deeply for Ken and I was thrilled that his dream and prayer would come true. But I was also full of panic. What would I really find, and how would we communicate?

For years Ken had isolated himself because of the difficulties communication presented. He was nearly a recluse in his home. The ear ringing had caused near total deafness, and one of his surgeries had also resulted in double vision which made the lip reading he had carefully learned a new struggle. How was I to believe we could possibly reach one another?

Then Ken had written me a wrenching postscript in his last letter "warning" me that he was neither courageous nor inspiring, and that physically he was not much to look at; he hoped I wouldn't be too disappointed. I wanted to die when I read those words. Reality had set in. This was going to be very hard. But I didn't want to disappoint *him*, and I prayed it would somehow be okay.

When I say that my heart was in my throat as our car approached Ken's home, I don't nearly convey how I was feeling—as if all the learned emotion of a lifetime was at full speed and volume. I also grieved that we were arriving an hour later than we were supposed to, since our taping had been delayed. Because Ken was alone in the home, there hadn't been a way to call and let him know. And I knew he'd planned to wait and watch by the door because he couldn't hear the bell or a knock. I wanted to die over that alone, the fact of having left him in a doorway, watching, for so long.

Beth came up to the house with me for the first introductions. Ken snapped a picture of us and Beth's antics and chatter distracted us both for those first few minutes. And it wasn't until she skipped her way back to the car that I really began to take Ken in: dark brown eyes almost invisible behind thick corrective lenses, a limp when he walked, his 5'10" height seemingly bowed under the blows of his life.

But his voice was strikingly well-modulated and his polite manner really attracted me. It wasn't a learned etiquette. It was true courtesy—that is, kindness and love for another. He was a gentle man, even if not one feature or movement would be labeled handsome or refined. Madison Avenue, I know, would call him homely, but they'd have been describing a face. You couldn't be in his presence and see just a face. He was worlds more—an incredible spirit which was only caged in a suffering body; he and his prison were very separate, and that was the agony.

We sat down opposite each other on a couch and began to talk. In two minutes I had forgotten myself and my fears completely. Ken was somehow managing to understand me. The conversation flowed. Only three or four times did we have to resort to the pad and pencil which Ken had reluctantly brought with him.

At the door, Ken had given Beth an adorable Kansas T-shirt. As with every gift he'd ever mailed to either of us, it was perfect, just what a six-year-old would think was "neat." He didn't just happen to find very appropriate gifts. I knew that. He studied people and listened and observed, and lovingly picked up all their clues until he arrived at *their* true wishes, not his own opinion of what would be nice or what they *should* like or want. The menu for dinner that evening included all my favorites. I couldn't figure out how he knew. His eyes shone as the meal progressed. Apparently if you investigate *Song for Sarah* you find clues to my likes and dislikes that I wasn't even aware were there. What a lesson! All of us leave such hints for eyes which really want to see us with the special sight of selfless love.

Ken was filled with questions and things he wanted to tell me. It was almost as though he'd rehearsed this interview over and over. And maybe he had. Although he never smiled I began to sense his wit and humor. Easily he had me laughing, and his own smile was in his eyes.

Eventually he began to talk about reading my book. Through his lengthy letters he had often tried to convey his sorrow for my own hurt which had touched him so deeply. He cried for me. He wished it had never been. And now, in person, he needed to re-explain how he'd felt he was a part of me and had hated my suffering. Incredibly, he felt it had been worse than his.

There was nothing remarkable about his actual

words, but there was something very unusual about the manner in which he spoke them. I had never, before or since, seen such compassion in a fellow human being's eyes. He sat there, wretched in his prison of pain, weeping within himself *for me.* If he could have, I knew he surely *would* have prevented my ever crying. Softly he said, "I cried and cried and cried. I loved Sarah too." That didn't make logical sense, but I knew it was true. And although this moment happened long after the historical fact of my accident, seven years later in that late February Kansas dusk, somehow—in retrospect—Ken was enabled to pick up my own grief and hold it for me, carry it a little bit of the way. Never, anywhere, have I felt such love.

I cannot explain it, nor can I forget it. That compassion healed something in my past, and that pain for my own grief was greater than my own. Ken, feeling forsaken by God, brought him to me.

There was so much more to that day. Ken opened doors and led me into his world. He talked about the noises he heard continually. It was not just ringing, but babies' screaming, pipes clanging, sometimes the sound of jets roaring inside of him. Often, he confessed, he would bang his head against the wall in despair. Day after day, night after night, for years . . . his inner being thrashed, screamed, and anguished, without a respite. And, not wishing to inflict his nightmare upon others, he withdrew more and more from them.

With animals he had found a gentle communion, and he'd had several special pets on his parents' farm. But through the years each animal had died. Ken's grief and anger left him unwilling to risk new loss, new hurt, by loving someone new. An angry self-protection.

When it grew dark Ken's brother and sister-in-law arrived from work. I didn't know where the afternoon had gone. I wished it had been longer, for even though I felt absolutely helpless in the face of his suffering, and I hated to see it, still it was good to be with him. All I had to offer him was the reality that I cared.

Later that evening Ken's family drove me back to my motel. As I rode along next to him in the back seat I felt bewildered—staring out the car window and asking why? of the black night. I thought of Beth, and health, and friends. I thought of my own worst day on earth. And I thanked God and really saw my blessings.

As Ken walked me to my motel door I was so angry with myself for forgetting, while I had the opportunity, to tell him that I loved him. Now it was too late. He couldn't hear me if I spoke the words, nor could he read my lips in the dark. I asked God to help me know what to do. And then as Ken thanked me and said good-bye, I found myself stretching my arms to him to cover his ears with my hands. He smiled (he understood) and I hugged him with all my love.

God, how I would have made his life different if I could have. But it wasn't given to me.

That night in my room I cried until I had dry heaves and could cry no more. But it was more than tears for Ken. It was tears for *all* pain, and for God who was right within Ken, but not yet found.

The very next morning Ken wrote to thank me for the visit. His last paragraph read:

Thank you for your kindness and loving concern from the beginning, and for bringing about a dream come true for me. And I especially want to thank you for something that touched me very deeply and which I'm so appreciative of: Thank you for hugging me.

New letters continued to arrive. And although they still contained pain and questions, they all carried a new excitement about friendship and love. Ken had entered a new world, and his enthusiasm was joyful. In the spring he asked if we could meet again, and I agreed. Ken's anticipation was full of the wonder of reaching out and letting in; he was finally finding his own appointed moments of beauty and letting them be.

But I only knew it through those last letters. That was to be all, for the very week we were to meet, Ken choked in his sleep and died. Finally, he was free.

When I began writing to Ken I think I felt, as he did, that most of his questions must somewhere have answers: If God can heal, and does sometimes dramatically heal, then why not always? Why didn't he heal Ken? Or end his misery by letting him die? All the *whys*.

But today I see that not all the *whys* deserve to be, should be, or will be, answered. Thinking that is so is man's desire, not God's promise. In fact, we will always live in a world of many unanswered *whys*, and somewhere along our journey that fact simply needs to be accepted. For to demand answers to every *why* is like seeking to know and control the wind. In spite of our wishes, it won't be channeled. That authority is not man's.

So I have placed many of my furious questions back onto my shelf. I am content that there are things I cannot know, and I am learning to concentrate on those I can. I am also sure that many answers, perhaps most, eventually come when we aren't even looking. One conclusion to Ken's story has come in that way even as I type these lines.

I suddenly see that Ken's intense search for God began years before we met. He read, he probed, he tested. He expected to find God by using his mental capacities, and he looked for him along the lines of rational questions and answers.

But I now understand that Ken was not able to find God through the intellect, for his keen mind's insistence on absolute understanding blocked the way. Absolute understanding is not given to humans. Even though God was hearing this man's prayer, there was a roadblock of his own making to its answer.

But God did not rest. Instead, he set about translating himself into a human form and emotion which someone like Ken *would* allow to meet his need. The body of Christ at work again. (The unexpected. The mystery.) And the form that he used was me, a loving friend. But it just happened to be me. It could have been anyone. The point is that God's overwhelming, relentless love, and his intent to answer sincere prayer, would not rest until he had translated himself into *some* form which Ken would accept.

I wonder how often he enters all our lives in shapes we aren't expecting? I wonder how often we cry to him and think we've missed him, but he is really right there. I think the answer is, every day.

I think back now to Ken's final weeks. He'd been so excited and full of joy. Really, his last letter had only been of love. And when he admitted love, he admitted God, and received the answer to his prayer.

I was filled with happiness when I saw it. Only my short sight, only my bondage to "the way things usually are" had prevented me from seeing it long ago. There are no limits to the shape of love. Or God.

Ken Harper died knowing God in every way but by name. And that didn't matter. He knows now.

I agree that I cannot, in many situations, perceive that love is at work ... but the proof of love is not in the laboratory or the logic class.—Leslie Weatherhead[6]

6
THE
RESOLUTION

I will never forget you.
I have carved you upon
the palms of my hands.
Isaiah 49:15-16

IN LATE JUNE OF LAST YEAR, fighting the feeling that mothers shouldn't really do this, should they? I took my first real vacation in a long, long time. No child. No speeches. No writer's deadlines. I was free.

I ended up in a part of the world that was new to me, the beautiful Caribbean. More than by all of its lush green charm, I was overwhelmed by its water. "Water for whose color there is no name," I kept repeating to myself. "Color for which there is no name." Not turquoise, not aqua, a blend of those, maybe, but brighter, more intense. God-painted.

There was no air conditioning and no need of it. Harbor breezes were swept inside the dining room of the resort by the thin blades of noiseless wooden ceiling fans, several of which dotted the ceiling and hung between green plants and brilliant blossoms. And from the center beam of the room's cathedral peak, tipped over and suspended by steel rods, hung a dark red canoe. Deep within its belly shone rustic lanterns, and one leaf-shaped, golden oak paddle.

At opposite ends of the room, and decorating the side railings were rich green palms. And everywhere outside the railings were more lush palms, banana trees, and nine-inch-wide leaves the size of fans which shaded the island grapes. Every yard and courtway was a fantasia of dense tropical growth. The whole atmosphere invited rest and laziness. It was just what I had sought.

My favorite spot was the breakfast porch, a small deck connected to the dining area by a canopied walkway. There, coffee was ground fresh each day and carried in old-fashioned white tin pots by smiling is-

landers. Somehow it tasted better for having been so
unceremoniously brought, and no one delivered it more
graciously than Leona, with her high, beautiful cheek
bones and wide black eyes.

It was in this setting, surrounded by wild rose-pink
blossoms, orange petals and the stately, swaying masts
of sea-going sloops, that I sought to renew my drained
energies.

I could write pages about the people I met there: Tall,
brown Llewellyn from whose chartered trimaran I snor-
keled in a coral reef and discovered a whole new world
under the world; Tracey and Joe Cloidt from Florida,
full of youth and openness and willingness to love; Bar-
bara and Frank Gill from Chicago, celebrating thirty
years of marriage, and radiating a joy in companionship
rare enough to seem make-believe. Everywhere were
beautiful lives to be known. But one life was to be more
important, for me, than the rest.

Charles Davies was a study in disarray. He walked
into my world at the salt-water pool, a beautiful oasis
set into the courtyard of the resort, on the Fourth of
July. My first image was of a cream-colored, suede L. L.
Bean hat, set determinedly atop a mop of long, sandy-
blond curls. His T-shirt boasted an advertisement for
Celestial Seasoning, and hung over cut-off cord jeans.
On his feet were worn, brown suede moccasins, on his
face a wild, reddish-blond mustache and beard, and in
his hand, an ever-present bottle.

He was a joyful drunk—but a drunk he certainly was.
Conversation with him was in snatches and all on his
terms. He seemed to take a particular liking to me and
followed me about. On that particular day a U. S. Navy

ship had moored in the harbor to give a twenty-one-gun salute in honor of the Fourth, so there were also several lonely sailors joining us "regulars" around the pool. Charles's exuberance sparked the sailors' good humor, and soon a celebration was in full swing. The party, conversation, and shared spirit of a holiday spent far from home lasted long into the evening.

For the next several days Charles was always around, always full of alcohol, but even in that state unable to hide a certain kindness which glowed in his eyes when he smiled. I fleetingly felt sorry that he wasn't willing to take the risk of life without all that liquid protection.

Then one morning, in a semi-sober state, Charles told one of the men in our poolside group that he drank continually to shut out the reality of twelve years ago, when, having had "one too many," he had caused an accident which took the lives of two people. Period. It was told in an offhand way, but the words screamed at me. They hurled me back into another summer, to the accident described in *Song for Sarah*.

August, 1974

... Almost there. Sarah squirmed. I asked "Would you like a cookie?" and as I turned around to reach your hand all I knew was a white car driving at us. My God.

And now, just like nothing, just like the earth, in a second, can be *not* the earth, they are telling me, "I'm so sorry." I'm looking into eyes full of pity and concern. I hear my voice giving phone numbers, telling names, reassuring strangers that I'm all right. ... Why is my mouth composed? ... Something hard is happening inside of me... Make it go away

... Horror like this can't find room inside of me. [7]
I went swimming to forget, but kept thinking about this
newly-revealed trauma. Charles was throwing his life
away because he felt so unforgivable. Voices screamed
inside of him. But I'd already lived in that land. Somehow I knew I had to reach him and make him know he
wasn't unforgivable. It wasn't so.

I supposed we'd both have to come halfway for me to
convince him, each of us willing to walk again through
our own fire. My family had been victims of a drunken
driver. He'd been a driver. He was the other side of my
pain. Yet how could we meet, how could any of this
happen, if he were never sober? How to bring it about
was beyond me. But I deeply desired it. And I prayed.

The following evening Charles was thrown out of his
room because of drunken behavior. It sobered him
momentarily; he literally had nowhere to go. Early the
next morning I came upon him as he wandered about
nervously, ashamed of himself and not knowing what
to do. At the moment he didn't dare drink. It was all too
clear that he couldn't control himself when he did.
Seeing that for once he was sober, I recognized my
chance.

Though I kept thinking "normal people don't do
things like this," I did it anyway—I asked him to walk
with me a short distance away from the pool. When we
were settled in a more private corner I told him what I
knew about him and what he needed to know about
me.

We'd not been one another's actual victim and per-
petrator, but it didn't matter. The situations were so
eerily similar that in that moment we were both sym-

bolic and literal; we stood for someone else and yet we were ourselves. I took his hand and told him that I forgave him and loved him. I said that if he'd been my own driver, the one who had demolished my car, my family, my life, it would have been the same. In the place of his victim, having all the right credentials, I absolved him.

We were not good and evil. Oppressed and oppressor. We were human. Survivors. People struggling to heal and live. We were both the same.

He pulled away and began to stride back towards the pool and safety. Tears were in his eyes and on his cheeks.

"I'm angry with you," he shouted, not turning back toward me, but looking stubbornly away. "You're making me hurt. I don't want to face these things. I can't stand the contents of my own mind."

"I know you hurt," I said softly. "But facing pain is the only way through it. Don't forget, I've been there too."

There was a long silence.

"I want to die," he said at last, still not turning around. I wasn't looking at him either.

"That's obvious. You're doing a good job of accomplishing it. Pretty soon you'll succeed."

"I served a year in jail. My wife left me. I've got an eighteen-year-old son I haven't seen since he was six."

"We could go on trading mistakes forever. My list is probably longer. The point is, in the face of death we both lived. *Lived.* We have to figure out what's left of our lives and why we have them."

I heard his footsteps, and once more he was sitting beside me.

"How on earth can you forgive me and say I'm lovable?" He looked right into my eyes.

"Because love is the final say, and it's real and it's true. Because I know the love of God. I want you to know it too."

We talked on and on. We talked of forgiveness and we talked of prayer. We talked, both of us, about asking *why* it happened. We hadn't wanted those accidents. We talked about trying to die—and about being afraid to live. We talked about needing love, but also about how frightening that was. How much easier it seemed to distance ourselves from life so that no one *could* love us, and open us up to further hurt.

We talked about other lives Charles might touch— and love—if he dared, lives he could "save" because of two lives now lost. We talked about searching for God and being loved by him no matter how badly we fail, and how he picks us up with love and believes in us, and how he allows us to learn, even through tragedy.

Charles reached for my hand and held it. It was one of life's rare links. A moment of fully-present love. Maybe just for an instant it was the kingdom of God. Probably I wasn't nearly ready to hold on to more, and so it couldn't be more.

During the three days which followed Charles did not drink. Everyone encouraged him and wondered at his change. But without prying they supported him. The man to whom he'd originally told his story counseled him for hours. Then as he sat with several of us around the pool one night he abruptly stood up and said goodbye. Carrying his worldly belongings in a blue zippered bag he left to take a seaplane to another island where he could make a new start.

I felt so sad and I wanted to run after him to say more —wish him a real farewell. But that would have been for my benefit. And so I stayed in my chair and didn't run anywhere. I let him choose the way which was easiest for him. Conversation continued around me, but I was far away inside wishing him well.

Two days later he reappeared at the poolside early in the morning. He borrowed a piece of paper and a pen and wrote me a letter which included these lines:

"My life seems to mean more to me now. I know it was all meant to be, meeting you. Paula, it was a real blessing to me and for me... I had to return to talk and see you once more. I'll never forget you.

Charles

P. S. I love you."

We talked about getting together the next day, my last on the island, but Charles never came. I didn't see him again.

I suppose I could speculate forever about his whereabouts or his present physical state. The part of me that is a trained counselor knows it is very unlikely such a pattern of drinking and drug-taking could be easily broken. It is difficult to turn a life around so quickly. Nevertheless the child in me hopes for miracles.

But even if there were none, one thing matters and gives all those hours value. At least for one moment of his life Charles had experienced love and forgiveness. That is not a small thing. As a matter of fact, that means there *was* a miracle. For both of us.

7
JULIE

*Fear not that your life
shall come to an end,
but rather that it shall
never have a beginning.*
John Henry Newman

THE YEAR EXISTS BECAUSE of its minutes, and every life, too. And some people live whole lifetimes never guessing that it is so. But our attitude toward the ordinary day is what determines the final statement we make with our life.

Three years ago in late, cold November I was asked to autograph books in Newtown, a pretty New England town in Connecticut's northwest hills. Proceeds from this Book Fair were being donated to a memorial fund set up in memory of Julie Judge, a young member of Newtown High's 1978 senior class. Following the Fair, Julie's parents and twin sisters welcomed me to their home, sharing with full hearts their recollections of their beautiful sister and daughter.

Julie's sisters remembered for me the inventive games they'd all played in childhood. Together they knew the special closeness of three sisters just two years apart in age, and their memories were of children's games of escape from hungry alligators, of dolls, sports, dance, and acrobatics. Unselfconsciously they "dressed up" and performed. Unwittingly, they matured and grew.

Julie grew in independence, unafraid of having her own ideas, and willing to face any resulting disappointments alone. But she loved equally to be part of things, never wanting to miss a minute of life, fitted in a kaleidoscope of living. Hers was a special spirit.

During Julie's teen years, music filled this vibrant home. She took piano and clarinet, and reluctantly relinquished her dreams of greater skills on the guitar because she was limited by small hands. Nevertheless she played for her mother, and at family gatherings, and sang in her school and church choirs as well.

The list of Julie's school honors is long: The D.A.R. award for the most outstanding junior student, the most popular senior girl, the most outstanding senior girl in athletics, cheerleader, Homecoming Queen, student council representative. Friends of both sexes were drawn by her magnetic personality. She warmly re ceived and also gave affection, and her ability to listen to and help others rose from the sensitive and caring spirit within her.

While some people struggle over every new skill or endeavor, Julie easily mastered most things she tried, not because she was naturally skilled in all things but because she possessed a spirit of determination to see things through. She said *yes* to life. She loved competition and challenge, cheered and warmed others like sunshine, and when she was absent from a special event, her absence was keenly felt.

Even in looking at photographs of Julie I felt her unique quality. There was a gift about her. I understood something of how she drew people. She drew me.

Her parents confessed to me that Julie's teen years, at least some of them, were tough. She hated the demands of curfews and family regulations, but eventually learned to accept them. Her greatest controls were her inner strengths.

Julie had a private dream; she wished to be truly outstanding in just one thing. In spite of the rainbow spectrum of accomplishments, her heart longed for what she termed a *real* talent, and her lack of one she considered to be a loss.

When Julie entered her church confirmation class she was not afraid to ask the hard questions, the *whys* and the *how comes*, which reinforced her faith when she found it. She taught Sunday school because she loved children and planned to work with them as a speech pathologist. Everyone wanted her to be their babysitter. And she knew that one day she'd be a mother with children of her own.

In the quiet haven of her room she was an avid reader. There she also listened intently to the confidences shared by her friends. And when alone she wrote about nature and the outdoors she loved. She loved crewel and needlepoint, and tried her hand at making candles. Vice president of her class, on the Prom Committee, water skier, editor of the yearbook, track team member, on the Superintendent's Advisory Board, high honors student, honors competitor in science fairs, earning honors in creative writing. Her seventeen-year-old self brimmed with life and achievement.

One cold February night in 1978, Julie and a boy friend called good-bye to her family as that evening's school basketball game closed. Her parents were there, as usual, to support the school team. Julie and Bob said they'd be back at her home shortly and then drove off to sit and talk for a while. They ran the car engine for warmth, unaware that the car had a faulty exhaust system which was clogged with snow from a drift as they parked. They never knew that it was carbon monoxide, and not oxygen that filled their air. Hours later their dead bodies were discovered.

Life and death both can come with no explanation. When a ninety-seven-year-old man, crippled with arthritis, dies in his nursing home, we are relieved. There's a rightness about it. His pain is over.

When a seventeen-year-old girl, vital with possibilities, dies for any reason, we are broken, and the outrage tears at one of life's unspoken assumptions—"If you live honestly and decently, your journey here will be good, long, and satisfying." But pain is blind and without conscience, and life is not always fair.

If we can't know about death, we'd best learn about life. We'd best know that it must be lived as if all we have is today.

In the play, *Our Town*, Emily is given the chance to return to earth for just one day after her death. She watches people living with such disregard for love and for others. Finally she agonizes,

"Don't people ever look at one another?"

Do we?

Do we pause to look around? Do we take time to live?

The value of life is not measured by one's longevity, but by the quality of one's love. Life is transient. Love is not. And so it is folly to live counting on tomorrow, and only that. Why do we resist shaping what we do have, the present?

Julie never waited for the right time to *really* begin living. She seized her present moments. She reached out to touch other people and allowed their lives to touch hers. She did not live protecting herself from life's possible hurts. She opened the door to joy, realizing that sadness enters by the same gate. But to protect oneself from sadness is to protect oneself from living, and from the joy.

Perhaps only by a measure of years could Julie's life be said to be found wanting. And that wanting, I think, is less than if she had stayed alive until advanced years but never had the courage to use all the raw materials of personality and talent with which she was born.

Too often it's not death that's the tragedy—it's the emptiness of life. Julie's life was something better than long. It was vital.

And that has made me want to tell her story, the story of someone I didn't even know. Her spirit, still alive in others, is for me the essence of the miracle of which we human beings can be a part. The importance of her few years is testimony to the way in which one life touches other lives and changes them. She is a small example of the interconnectedness of everything living.

We have already witnessed the frightening effects of our twentieth-century ways on the environment of this planet. How far-reaching *are* our acts? Who can say? Perhaps we affect the paths of the stars. But this at least is certain, that who we are changes the life around us. If we choose to be loving, involved, withdrawn, cold, critical, judgmental—we shape the world in some way. Life is, at once, gift and responsibility. Everything matters everywhere.

And Julie, whom I never knew, changed me.

8
THROUGH
THE
VALLEY

The wind blows wherever it wishes;
you hear the sound it makes,
but you do not know where it comes from
or where it is going.
John 3:8

With God, all things are possible.
Mark 10:27

"YEA THOUGH I WALK THROUGH THE VALLEY of the shadow of death..." That verse of Scripture, for me, had always been a clear reference to someone's bodily death. I'd heard it recited at funerals since I was a young child. To me it seemed to carry the hope that when others die and we necessarily grieve, God is still with us and will lead us to the acceptance and understanding of such pain.

But that child's knowledge was limited. In fact deaths come all through life, every day. And they often have little to do with dying people. They are the deaths of ideas, hopes, dreams, relationships. They are deaths caused by aging and loss of mobility, by job loss and early retirement, by diseases which limit us, by our own walls (erected to protect us, so we think, from the things we fear).

But it was my friend Paul Everett who stretched my own understanding of David's "valley" of death in Psalm 23. He did so unexpectedly as we lunched together in Pittsburgh one day. I was there to speak at the Pittsburgh Experiment which Paul heads, and we had stolen a few hours beforehand to discuss my talk and a radio broadcast we would do the next morning. Eventually the conversation settled into some of our personal feelings about heartache and trial. It prompted Paul to tell me some new feelings he had about "walking through the valley."

What he suggested was that in the analogy of the shepherd and sheep it was significant that the sheep were taken to higher and lower pastures through the valleys. These valleys contained the best vegetation and water but were also filled with predators and difficulties. Yes, the shepherd stayed with the sheep through the difficult valleys. But it was also he who had led them there. In the same light, not only will God accompany us through the hard, stark valleys, but sometimes he may even *lead* us to them in order for us to attain a joy we could receive in no other way. Such paradox again—joys arrived at only through tears.

In May, 1982 I stood, unknowingly, at the edge of such a valley. If it had been up to me I know I'd never have freely taken even one step toward it. Every instinct told me to protect myself and my heart. I could see no possible joy ahead. But the truth is, we seldom can. Maybe that's because we aren't given eyes which flawlessly discern true delight. We are often deceived. But we *are* are given hearts and souls which yearn for truth, and which will, when we're finally willing, be more afraid of running from life than of facing it.

In the end, that's how those who are free become free. They are the few who learn that truth, not pleasure, is the hiding place of joy.

The particular valley of which I write concerns the automobile accident in which I'd been involved seven years before. I'd fought a hard fight since then and had learned to believe in life again—even life with all its risks. I had built myself a new foundation, and I didn't ever want my house shaken again.

But life is not so neat, nor is it always respectful. Instead it seems to be "what happens to us while we're making other plans." Thus it was without consideration for all my strenuous adjustments and all my fears, that I

started down the entry ramp to a new highway. And I
confess it never occurred to me that it might have been a
way to which I was being led, and along which I could
be changed for the better. I felt only as we usually do
when confronted with something unknown and fear-
some: I wanted to be allowed to have another way.

But I was wrong, and with hindsight I can now embrace that valley. God took me there knowingly, I'm so
sure. I only regret that I couldn't have trusted him from
the start.

The following pages are journal excerpts from the
valley that took the form of a five-week court trial resulting from the accident which claimed my husband's
and daughter's lives. Our legal suit claimed negligence
on the part of the state for failure to erect a metal barrier
(whose need had been recognized by the state but
which had never been put in place) along the section of
grassy median which divided the interstate highway.
This failure to provide the protection that highway
safety precautions demanded allowed a drunken
motorist to hurtle across unimpeded, striking our car
and causing the fatal injuries.

This external circumstance—the trial—was the
easiest part. Internally it meant I would be moving into
the dark distances of my soul, reliving the worst heartache and confusion I'd ever known.

September, 1978, Preliminaries
The beginning. I met with my lawyers today to "get
ready." The truth is that though they're ready I will
never be. This isn't very real to me yet, and there's com-

fort in the knowledge that this trial is still months, maybe years ahead of me. I can successfully ignore anything
that far distant.

March, 1982
My sitter's messages today included this one: CALL
ATTY. RICHARD BIEDER. As soon as I read it I decided to ignore it. It will be about my trial and I don't
want to hear it. If it's so terribly urgent I guess he'll call
back.

April, 1982
Richard Bieder called and got me. In ten short minutes
his voice of authority was rearranging my life.
    "The trial is about to begin."
    "How coincidental," I laughed. "I'm leaving for Flor-
ida. I can't make it."
    He chuckled, and in the chuckle plane tickets and
sunshine were cancelled. Lesson number one in things
legal: I would be doing the adjusting. Very unhappily I
changed my plans.
    I would rather do anything else than face this trial.

April 30
Richard comes to see me today because my recent flu
has left me too weak to drive to him. He takes notes as
he makes an outline of my once-upon-a-time life. He
searches out pictures and probes me for memories. I'd
love to hate him for this, but I can't seem to work up
any resentment. Actually he is very nice. Sometimes he
even makes me laugh. But once he leaves I feel very

sober again. No amount of humor completely covers the wounds.

May 5
I've been assigned a list of things to do. But it's far from simple. I am asked to walk into my memories and pull out faces and names. I sense the beginning of something hard.

For two days I call, and trace, and work non-stop on my assignments. My heart resists me every inch of the way. I don't want to go back down this road. What if it starts to own me, as once it did? What if I'm not strong enough to stand it?

May 19—*Day One.*
Selecting a jury. I once studied this in an eighth grade civics class and I've listened to many news broadcasts. I worked in my father's law office one summer. But the privilege of this country's lawful system never struck me as it has today.

I can't resist imagining the life of each prospective juror. All strangers, but within a few weeks they will be my intimates, familiar with the details of my life. And these strangers will finally pronounce the justice or injustice of conditions which robbed me of the building materials of my dreams.

I know very well that life sometimes mates people in curious ways. Sometimes lives touch only briefly. But what we do with such moments is a burden to which we'll forever be answerable. We rule our moments.

Time and decisions seem even more dramatic here.

None of us has ever met, and if I do see a juror on the street now, we can't speak, not even a hello. A smile might be misconstrued. And yet it is they who will judge my claim, and possibly influence my fate.

I wonder what they're thinking and how they feel when they look at me. Who will be fair and who will not? Who cares? Who wishes they were back at work? Who thinks it's a lark?

May 20

For a while I got caught up in my lawyer's skill in deciding whether or not to accept a potential candidate for the jury. Sometimes he is convinced the second the person walks in. He is considering many elements—age, nationality, marital status, profession, sex. At the end of the second weary day of interrogations I am tired of considering anything. I'm just sorry for all of us that we're here.

But tonight, just before 5 P.M., we finally have it.

A jury of my peers.

May 20

I don't feel ready for this. The necessity to enter this court is really an edict forcing me to face roads inside of me where I don't want to travel.

I fear what I will feel. When the lawyers' harsh realities rearrange the furniture of my heart, worn places will show. And I am vulnerable where I am worn.

I cannot look back only with my mind for their testimonies. My heart comes with me. We cannot separate.

I look into the eye of all that once was me, and the

sadness is there, waiting. I anguish that it has all been
so. "I'm sorry," I say into the black night. "I am very
sorry. I didn't mean for it all to be. I didn't ask for it. I
didn't wish that they would die. I'm sorry I lived."

"I'm sorry I wasted so many days of my past. I'm
sorry I wasn't smarter about what gives life meaning."
All I feel are my tears. I haven't wanted to cry again—
ever. I haven't wanted to open these doors.

They weaken me, these rooms I haven't visited in so
long. I feel their strain like an iron hand and I cannot
fight it. It is bigger than me.

My one hope is this. If I make this journey, then perhaps one day there may no longer be these walls inside
of me. I would like my heart to be free.

May 25
Something inside me flinches every time they read
"The case of Paula D'Arcy versus the State of Connecticut", or when they repeat again and again, "August 18, 1975 and the tragic accident which claimed the
lives of ..."

My very real, flesh-and-blood life has become a public argument. I feel publicized and yet ignored. They
discuss me as though I weren't a person. I'm a number
—a court case.

May 26
I can rally myself to endure two days of court in a row,
but when the third day begins I find I am slipping. Too
many memories and too little respite. Sometimes I cry
myself to sleep, I don't even know why. I *am* over all of

this, aren't I? Didn't I already wage this battle and win? Could I possibly have to re-fight my life's worst war?

May 26
I've never seen the pictures of the crash till now. It's strange, like watching a scene that both is and is not my life. Richard takes me to lunch with the crash reconstruction expert. He tells me how unlikely were my chances of surviving.

Back in court, while they argue about tire treads and velocity, I am glued to the photographs of smashed green metal. Always before my question has been, "Why did I live?" Now it's a more frightening question: "How?"

May 27
One of the realities of a courtroom trial is an astonishing series of delays. I rest my head on my elbow and think about the horrifying waste of tax money: a delay for witness interrogation.

A delay because the judge is hearing pre-trial arguments for *another* case in his chambers. A delay because lawyers and/or witnesses are late.

I don't want to be here in the first place and now I am wasting hours of each day. The only thing that happens on time is adjournment. Usually.

May 28
Behind me sit a row of friends who've come to support me. They come every day. How could anyone be so lucky? They encourage me that I am not alone. They

encourage me that even though this fight is in my name, they have added theirs.

I hear continually, by postcard, from my friend Jane White. I tuck her messages of support in my purse, and when I think I can't stand the dissection of my life any longer, I take one out. Reading her words steadies me.

Then sometimes at night my concerned friend Greg will call long distance from New York. He does for me what becomes so hard for me to do for myself when I am in the grip of my emotions: he puts my life back in perspective. He says, "You've already won this fight. They can't take away all your acceptance of fate, and all your adjustments. This is momentary now. It is a *re-living*, not living." How much that helps!

My friends bear a powerful gift. They believe in me. Today they are the arms of Christ around me, upholding and comforting me.

May 31

The day I fear the most is approaching fast. The drunken driver who struck us will be brought to court by the state, and I most definitely do not want to meet him. I have never wanted to meet him. It's been a help to have him faceless all these years. I can forgive a blank and I've tried to. But the awful truth I ask myself is, can I forgive a face?

June 1

Today was spent exposing my past financial life. I thought last week's intimate testimony of friends and family would be hard. I ached at the tender remem-

brances many students shared about Roy. It accentu-
ated the loss of his life and left me in no doubt that it
was senseless. He was a man full of future. It didn't
make me cry for me; I cried Roy's own tears for him.

But even that pain didn't match sitting in that courtroom today while they diagrammed my life in terms of
dollars. Expenses, expenditures, and savings. Every
small, private, personal detail. I kept thinking, it's like
what's done when someone dies. But I'm alive.

And then I despair that they have a right to discuss
this at all. They discuss it because, in a court of law, it
makes a difference whether the deceased was an IBM
executive or whether he cleaned streets. It comes to
that. When do we begin to see one human life as un-
equal to another? And what happens to civilization
when we do?

June 2

Today the police officer who was at the scene of our
wreck gave his testimony. Some bizarre law says that
evidence of the victim's pain and suffering (e.g., moan-
ing, crying) allows a jury to consider an even greater
cash award.

The hideousness of that sweeps through every cell in
me. What man believed that? What body of legislators
became convinced and confirmed it? What happens to
people that we so little understand life as to begin to
define it in such terms?

He described our bodies, the dead and the living, and
the broken glass. I sat there. But when he said that
Sarah was whimpering, I was beaten. I cried all that
day. They offered to recess, and my lawyer compas-

sionately put his arm around my shoulder. He said we could adjourn.

But I had no intention of stopping. We'd only have to begin again, and it wouldn't be any different. I just wanted to finish. So I told them to proceed. But no matter what I did or how hard I tried, I couldn't stop crying.

June 2

The periods of escape aren't big enough for me. I need a week off. But now, in addition to my day in court, are the interviews and sessions with witnesses in the evening. Stories. Pictures. Photo albums. Home movies. My old life won't leave my direct line of vision.

I am becoming so sad. Now I don't just cry myself to sleep. I cry even before I reach home. I've driven my car, at 15 miles per hour, into two parking lot poles.

I'm bridging two worlds, yesterday and today, and I'm not making it.

How on earth can a previously completed road be re-traveled? Can grief hide itself so well, even for years?

Several years ago I was sure that there were no tears left inside of me. But now I guess that's wrong; no pain is ever totally *over*. We always carry our wounds, even the healed ones. A time or a place may at times regenerate our sadness. But it's a re-living, not a living, as Greg wisely assures me.

And it's a sign, I think, that there's more grief work to be done. Deeper work. Funny how grief will find you. You can postpone it, but you can't eradicate it. If it's not faced and brought out through tears, it assumes differ-ent shapes. Fears. Defenses. Being afraid to love or be loved. Anger. Hostility. Resentment. Bitterness. And in time these wound more deeply than the first hurt, often without our knowing it. And we may fail to identify them as suppressed grief at all.

In the long run, I guess tears are really the kindest way.

June 3

The state argued today about the degree of my loss. Comparisons to other tragedies were made. My head ached. They are weighing something that can't be weighed.

If you lost your arm and I lost my family, is my loss necessarily greater or less than yours? What a horrible question. I only know that all the pain you can bear at a given time is equal to all the pain I can bear. Period.

We should be weeping about pain, not measuring it.

June 3

The drunken driver who struck us was racing with another car. Tomorrow the driver of the second car will appear. I dread it.

June 4

Henry Nichols. I don't know if he was different than I'd imagined because I can't remember now what I ever thought he'd be. I only know that seeing him this morning made my past seem very real. This is not a story I've told or heard. These were real people and this really happened.

It cut through my life and changed it. It hurt me. It made me want to die.

But when I saw the second driver today I faced an awful truth: it didn't matter to him at all. His passengers had lived. Mine didn't. "So, tough luck, lady," his whole attitude and appearance screamed at me. He shrugged, "That's the breaks."

I think he was drunk, even in court. At any rate he wouldn't cooperate. His blood/alcohol level at the time of the crash was 0.13%. Legal intoxication is reached at a level of 0.10%. But he testified that he didn't even think he'd been drinking.

Previous witnesses, still with fear in their voices, had testified that he'd passed them that day "like lightning." Their cars had been shaken by his speed. But he said he was going 55 miles per hour.

What kind of world is this? How do human beings, so full of potential at birth, ever turn so far away? I wanted to die watching him. He sat and laughed at my pain.

Unwanted thoughts kept finding me: "Roy and Sarah, in all their tenderness and love, died. And he lived."

My minister was in court that day, as he'd been so many times. I felt cold, and whipped from the inside out. I felt stretched. And I told him as he gave me the hug I needed, that the last hour when Nichols testified had tested every shred of Christianity I ever felt I had. Because from deeper than the terrible bitterness and resentment which had hold of me, came a voice which said, "In my eyes, neither Roy nor Sarah are greater than he."

June 4

When I was expecting Sarah I was an ardent follower of Watergate events and people. It became so easy to label all lawyers deceitful, and the judicial system a sham. It was as easy as it always is to look at a small piece of anything and conclude that all other instances will be similar. With one sweep we can write off faces and never see how self-righteous we've become.

So if for nothing else, I'm glad I'm having this experience in order to change my prejudice about courts and law and self-serving lawyers. I think my lawyers were hand picked for me; their sensitivity and caring surprises and also sustains me. This has become more than a stark legal suit in a formal courtroom. There are human beings here who believe in one another. Win or lose, that's a prize.

June 4

The faces of my jurors will probably never leave me. I pray for each of them every morning as we begin. But that's not because I wish them to award me a favorable verdict. It's that I know what a fine line there is, always, between my condition in life and anyone else's. But for life's infinite web of chance, our positions across this room could have been reversed.

I pray for the clerks and sheriffs, the witnesses, the judge, my lawyers, and the state's attorneys. I imagine this room surrounded by love. Somehow it seems that perfect justice can't be dispassionate.

June 4

This morning I will tell my lawyer I can't go through with this any more. Last night before supper Beth threw a rock and broke one of our windows. That rock was her outcry. "Why aren't you ever home any more, Mommy?"

My sister Barby just left and now my sister Anne is here helping me. But I'm not me.

Here I am, sobbing because of losses I've already accepted. How is that? There is no loss of faith, no distrust of God. I know he's with me. It's just that re-living the pain makes it too real again. Even faith can't spare us tears. But my decision to stop facing this madness could end them.

June 4

Yes, that's the best plan. I must stop all this. But my attorneys were caught in traffic this morning and there was no time to speak to them before court. Then lunch break. No time again because of research which needed to be done in the court library. During the afternoon our own expert witness on median barriers, Dr. Bob Brenner, arrived from the Institute of Safety Analysis in Washington, D.C. At first I listened because there was nothing better to do. But soon his fierce conviction caught me in its momentum and started to defuse my resolve to quit. Just when I was going under, our own witness handed me back my purpose.

You see, there is no victory for me personally in this court. I can't win. I lost seven years ago. But my battle today *can* make a statement that makes a difference for someone else. The life of some unknown individual, some loving family. Crippled as I feel right now, I know the battle is worthy. For what good is *my* life if I think and act as if no one else's life matters?

I'm changed. I *won't* tell my lawyers to withdraw the case, even if I sit here and cry, because if we win, the state will begin to erect the required median barriers *before* people die, and not after. Somebody else may never have to be me. I can stand it for that.

June 5

I cannot believe how well versed my lawyers have become concerning the details of my life. They know things about me that *I* don't. They refer to my cousins and friends on a first name basis. They've listened, heard, and remembered things Roy wrote, thought, and said that I had forgotten. Who'd have guessed this would be part of the process?

June 5

I sense that there is another, hidden trial going on here. I think the legalists silently name it "Pacification vis à vis an award of money." At least that's how I feel every day when the state urges my lawyer to have me stop proceedings now and consider settling out of court. As I refuse, they continue to offer higher and higher figures.

Even the judge, through my lawyer, urges me to settle. He tells him that when the case is over he'll go home, the jury will go home, *everyone* will go home but me—I'll never go home. And so he feels that there should be some compensation in this for Beth and me. Some security.

I start to wave away this kind of argument, but Richard makes me listen. He forces me to look at facts. And they're hard.

I knew from the start that we weren't favored to win. Suits against the state (like city hall) don't have a successful track record. And in this case it is our burden to prove that the state's negligence about the median barrier was the accident's sole cause. That task isn't simple. There are many other circumstances which the state has fingered and claimed.

I've listened to Richard. His argument has been that regardless of other circumstances, for example drinking, speed, weather conditions, car failure, *whatever*, a car cannot cross a flat, unobstructed, grassy median if the required protective barriers are there. The argument is true, it makes sense, and we both believe in it.

But can a jury, sworn not to be emotional, also make that mental assent? All the past records say no. Statistics tell me that our chance of winning is only 20 percent.

Twenty percent. So if I let this verdict go to a jury, I can expect to walk home, broken by enduring it all, my pockets filled only with wonderful motives and ideals. "You've got to think it over," Richards insists.

Well, I know this much right away. In an unsafe world, we have to care for and protect one another. I know that my state acknowledged the need for a barrier at the site of the accident when the highway was still being built. But someone cut a corner. And only with a favorable verdict can I put any pressure on those who cut such corners. That's the only reason I'm sitting here in the first place.

June 6

I've mulled over whether or not to settle out of court for several days. Tomorrow morning is my last word. I can't sleep. I can't even sit still. I never paced up and down before in my life.

Am I being really foolish? Aren't you mentally ill if you refuse hundreds of thousands of dollars? Probably. Am I being selfish? What about Beth? With one word I could insure her future education, and then some. We'd never have to worry or strain financially again. I'd never again be short of money for groceries or gas. We'd have a new freedom.

As it is I've just taken my hard-saved down-payment for a badly-needed new car and used it instead to take advantage of a once-in-a-lifetime chance to buy a small beach cottage that Beth and I both love. What a risk that was, and I could make it safe in a second.

I could have sure cash tomorrow. And part of me says *go for it*. Do good with it. You deserve it. Listen to what everyone is saying.

I wonder if they are really right. I bet they're all sleeping soundly right now. But I can't sleep.

I keep begging God for guidance, but I know I'm not stopping long enough to hear it. I keep on pacing.

In my mind I act out two possible scenes from my future.

Scene One: I am sitting next to sixteen-year-old Beth, and I take her hand. "I know, Beth, that you've deeply missed having a father and sister all these years. But, strangely, their deaths did provide for us. And now I can afford to give you every opportunity."

Scene Two: I am sitting next to sixteen-year-old Beth, and I take her hand. "I know, Beth, that you've deeply missed having a father and sister all these years. Their deaths didn't have to be. Men were negligent. The only recourse I had was a trial by jury, and I believed in that. We were lucky for it, in this land. When it works well and even when it does not, it does try to be fair. I know we struggle today. But *I couldn't compromise what I believed in.* And I hope you never will, either."

I like Scene Two infinitely better, and I feel myself growing quieter. Paul Fanelli calls to see how the day has gone. I tell him about the question of settling. "Don't you see?" he says, "You've never needed money more, so what better time to be tempted by it?"

He's right. He's very right. My muddled thoughts cohere into real clarity. "Wherever your treasure is, there shall your heart be also."

June 7

Today at noon recess Richard and his associate, Alex, and several of my friends and I left for lunch. But the busy restaurant couldn't seat all of us at one table, so Richard and I sat separately. I was glad, because I had a lot to say to him.

Over quiche and fish I told him of my irrevocable determination to see this thing through. I would consider no more offers. I recounted for him my two "scenarios for the future" with Beth. I also said that I clearly saw the odds and how they were stacked against me. I explained that I could not live only trusting something halfway. I'd rather pick up pieces than be controlled by my fears. Facing them makes life very, very hard, but much more worthwhile. The elusive prizes like joy and freedom never come without high stakes and great risk. Freedom is expensive.

I think I talked an awful lot. It was so clear to me that the guarantee I was putting my trust in—namely, God —was way beyond winning or losing. And the less I am ruled by fear, the closer I am to him.

Richard took it all in quietly with not one attempt to persuade me otherwise. I painfully knew that a settlement guaranteed him a handsome fee. A loss, should my fight for this principle fail, meant not one cent of recompense for five years of detailed preparation. He only said, "I am with you all the way."

It was the chance in a million that we could do some good for mankind: Someone else might not have to be me. I believed in that more than the world's securities. And from that moment on, we'd won. Win or lose in court, we'd won.

June 8

Today I learned that dirty tricks in courts of justice are not confined to "Perry Mason" or "The Defenders." I cannot believe some of the wheelings and dealings I see. Three times this week we've come close to having a mistrial declared. Since there are no alternates left on the jury, we would have to re-try the case from the beginning if anyone gets sick. That is an impossibility. I only have it in me to go through this one time.

The defense attorney hammers me with questions which I cannot answer. I look like a fool. I repeat "I don't remember," a hundred times. I ask to be able to explain why I don't remember and am told loudly, "Just answer the question."

Does the jury understand anyway? Do they see that the first three months following the accident were—are —a total blank for me? I'm not being deceitful. If my signature is on the papers they shove before me then "Yes," I must have signed them. But "No," I have no memory of ever having seen that paper before in my life.

I feel shaky and defeated. My mood swings are too swift. Everything against me is bigger than me. After a short recess my friend Bev slips me a small brass disc. On it some words are engraved: "No weapon formed against you shall prosper" (Isaiah 54:17).

That turns me around. I feel calmer. When you recognize the enemy, he loses some of his power.

June 9
I feel very nervous this morning. The trial has worn me down more than I thought it could. I am remembering things I don't want to remember, and am being forced to face things I wish weren't there. I feel so full of anger. Sorrow always needs something to blame.

And yet what is ever gained by fleeing pain and running the other way? I devoted too much of my earlier life to that false chase. It means you're never free, for you can't be free and hiding at the same time.

Sometimes at night I cry for broken dreams. But I won't live in them. There are always new dreams, if life is what a person reaches for. Life can't defeat you without your consent. Why do we think we can dream only one dream?

Anyway, tears are better than the finest "control." They do something which masks cannot. They heal.

June 10

"You need to be strong today," Richard tells me. "The driver who struck you will testify this morning."

Why is it so scary to finally meet him? I long ago wanted to forgive him, and I think I have. I pray for him every day. Am I not confident that Christ in me has forgiven him and forgotten his deed? That's the promise. So why am I in panic?

I know why. It's because maybe when I meet him face to face I won't feel the way I wish I could. Maybe I'll hate. Maybe I'll say right out loud, "You are the flesh-and-blood instrument of all this. *You!*"

I cannot bear to face this and yet I cannot run. Two months passed between nine o'clock and eleven. And then at eleven-thirty he was ushered in. I know the room was crowded, but for me we two were the only ones there.

He was small, and handsome, I thought, with deep brown eyes. I wondered if there were Indian blood in his ancestry because of his fine, almost chiseled, features. Why was I calmly thinking such superficial things? They tried to keep me from feeling. But they didn't have the power. The physical appraisal was momentary and it would never matter. But what happened next did, for something extraordinary happened.

I was looking at the same features and yet beginning to see this man in a wholly different way.

As I looked into his eyes, a new awareness found me. Instead of being blinded by my own hurt, all I saw was *his* fear and pain. It was so real that it filled me and I ached for him. No outward expression of his betrayed any sorrow. But I saw it. By some miracle I was seeing beyond his face and finding the self he could not show.

Slowly I realized that I was not, as I'd always felt, the only survivor. We were both survivors. The two of us. And my worst feeling, the haunting aloneness of being the only one left, disappeared forever in that moment. Contradiction—but truth—the incredible fact that *he* should be the answer to that or any of my pain.

Equally unreasonable was the fact that as our eyes continued to meet I began to see that his pain was worse than mine. Was I crazy to feel that? But I knew it. If I could have, I would have picked up his pain for him and carried it forever. And I hoped against hope that the love which filled me was somehow reaching him through my eyes. His hurt was naked to me, it was so plain.

I knew what was happening, and I sighed deeply. I was experiencing what it is like to see another man through Christ's eyes, and in that experience to be only accepting, and to have forgiveness which withholds no love. It had become my nature to love him.

What irony. I'd always assumed that the party to be forgiven was the one who received forgiveness' mighty power. But it's not so. Instead it was *I* who was being let go, released—I who had been the prisoner.

June 10

It's night time. I keep thinking what power there is in forgiveness coupled with love. Years ago, when I prayed to forgive, I surely felt none of this power. It doesn't come instantly, and its power shouldn't be measured according to time, I now see. The full feeling of forgiving is not its first sign.

I guess forgiveness, like true love, is first a commitment of the will, not a feeling. It's obedience, something we choose to do. And that first step, wanting it, is the hardest. And we must include God; we're just not big enough to handle it alone.

And it costs. From the moment of wanting to forgive we give up our mental rights to tangle angrily with that person anymore. We commit our thoughts to new dwelling places. We command our minds and lips to inhabit new worlds, not old. And only long, long after these resolutions comes the "feeling."

When we leave justice (the righting of wrong, hurts, the retribution) to him, God plants within us the seed of actually *feeling* forgiving. That's the sequence, and that's the necessary beginning for complete healing. Forgiveness is an irreplaceable characteristic of real love.

What a strange day. That drunken driver was the last person on earth I expected to teach me anything at all about what real love is all about. I thought he was the instrument in my life through which love had been taken from me. But he was precisely the one whom God used to replace it in greater measure. Mystery.

I see what the trouble is with us. Our expectations

hold us captive. And as a result we don't begin to imagine, or believe, what is possible with God. We spend years looking in life's reasonable, but wrong places. And so we don't recognize our real teachers. We don't feel the wind of the Spirit in our faces.

June 11
Psalm 23. "He has prepared a table before me in the presence of mine enemies. My cup runneth over." Love often breeds pain. But pain can also introduce love. That's the potential of every resurrection we allow.

Yesterday, after everyone left the darkened court room, I walked back in alone. I stood before the witness stand where my enemy had stood. And I closed my eyes and thanked God that seven years ago, within that mass of crushed steel and spilled blood and broken glass, I had lived.

I was aware now that even in the madness of that disaster, God had been present. I believe his eyes simultaneously saw not only the accident and the strewn bodies, but also the potential for this healing many years later, if *I'd* let it be.

What a gift it is to be able to trust that every similar highway (nightmare) contains him and his potential resolution, through love. I wanted it. And I sincerely prayed (knowing full well the horrible risk of loss which love contains) that I would never be afraid to love, or to be loved. Otherwise, what meaning is there in life?

When I got back outside I ran. I ran and ran, laughing. I was free.

June 17

It was warm today, like summer. I dressed nervously, knowing that today the jury was to bring in their verdict. I came armed with a book and some writing that needed to be done, but I couldn't concentrate on either. Ironically, after five weeks of loving and constant support by so many friends, no one was able to join me this morning. So by myself I did something very profound: I sat and stared at the floor, wringing my hands. I simply didn't know what to do with the anticipation.

Even Richard was nervous, but he was occupied with another client in a small waiting room. Alex was busy in the court's library. After a while, Adam, the friend and lawyer who'd first filed this suit for me came in through the swinging doors. He looked quickly at the door behind which the jury was deliberating. I shook my head "no," and he sat down beside me and inspected the floor too.

Minutes passed, and suddenly the jury room door shot open. Or maybe the door opened and *I* shot up. The jury foreman grimly told the sheriff, "Tell the judge we're ready."

Adam pushed me to my seat at the lawyer's table and within minutes the court filled. Lawyers, clerks, and stenographers came running, spilling into the benches. Everyone was anxious to witness the climax of the "impossible" case.

I whispered to Richard beside me, wanting to know if I had to stand when they read the verdict. "You're not on trial for murder!" he assured me with a grin and a hug. "Just sit."

The judge arrived and the jurors filed into their box. Their faces were impassive; they couldn't be read. I felt like doomsday. I shot a look back at Adam and he rolled his eyes. "This is crazy," I said to myself, "this tilting at windmills." It takes too much out of a person.

In the lull I took one long, last look at those dear jurors. I will never forget any of their faces. No matter what they had decided, I thanked them silently for interrupting their lives to take seriously matters such as democracy, and justice, and my life. I prayed that none of them would ever be afraid, or alone. I thought of how our lives had touched so deeply, and yet we've never spoken one word directly to one another. But who ever said that might not be so? Richard Bach said: "The bond that links your true family is not one of blood, but of respect and joy in each other's life. Rarely do members of one family grow up under the same roof."

And Jesus: "Who is my mother and who are my brothers?" and stretching out his hand—he said, "Behold, my mother and my brothers. For whoever does the will of my father who is in heaven, he is my brother and sister and mother."

Now it was time. Richard had an arm around me; so had Alex. With rising inflection the foreman of the jury was saying, "We find for the plaintiff, Paula . . . !"

What a moment! We three friends gasped a breath as one, and grinned at each other across the table. You could have felt it only if you'd been one of us. We'd done it. We'd really done it. It was more than a verdict. It was justice. She was ours.

I was hugged by more lawyers that afternoon than I

probably ever will be again. The place was crazy with excitement. It wasn't the false high of drugs or liquor. It wasn't forced laughter at a dull party. It was the exhilaration of real joy. And love.

And my heart heard, from somewhere, "The one who honors me will I honor." I tried to talk to people, and I was crying. My tears were joy and pain, all together. I couldn't stop them, and I didn't want to. They were all the places I'd been. And where I was now. They were me.

June, 1982
The ending. Afterwards, Richard and Alex and Adam and I laughed together over champagne and lobster. We called everyone we knew. We told people we didn't know. We held on to every minute of the day.

But neither joy nor tears can keep a day from slipping. Time will never be held, nor slowed, nor rushed. Only our hearts, at times, make it seem so. And so even as we thought we held it, time was edging us forward, purposefully, to tomorrow.

Saying goodbye to Richard and Alex was the only sadness to mar the day, and it was as great as the joy, for they had become a part of me. We'd been in strange lands together, but now it was time to go home, and go on. Nobody else who'd not been a part of it would ever know exactly how it had been. That's how memories are, they are the gifts of those who own them.

So only we three knew, when we parted, what it had

been, and we wrapped it up as ours. We lingered. Beginnings and endings are both hard, not being separate at all. One contains, and requires, the other. But in between are wonderful gifts of friendship. And believing in something. And someone.

And we were all changed by the shared moments, and carried away a bit of the other. That's how love is.

9
THE
BETRAYER
THAT
IS US

*He who does not love
does not know God.*
1 John 4:8

ABOUT A MILE AWAY FROM OUR SUMMER COTTAGE is a simple,
white frame church, so ordinary in outward appearance
that I can't imagine seekers of beauty even slowing
down, much less stopping, to look inside.

But they are fooled. For in contrast to its plain exterior
the church boasts a beautiful secret: an interior filled
with arches of rich, polished beams whose dark,
wooden tracery stretches upward in a magnificent
cathedral peak.

As I sit below, I often imagine myself encased by
generations of oak, and I think they must be proud,
somehow, to form this canopy for a holy meeting place
with God. I think of Luci Shaw's poem, "Behind the
walls," and her lines,

Where others notice siding, shutters, paint,
I shall see behind the walls
the secret trees
standing straight and strong
as pines in the free groves outside. [8]

And in my own heart I wonder about all that the trees
know, including the real meaning of freedom.

Sunday mornings the church's long sanctuary over-
flows, tourists and beach residents spilling into every
aisle, many forced to stand. Such crowds, compounded
by the humid heat of July and August, cause anything
but a relaxed, receptive congregation and I pity those
who must preach sermons.

But one hot July Sunday the words which were given
transformed themselves beyond punctuated sentences
into what moves and heals: they became God's message. It would be hard to know if the miracle happened
for everyone, for just a few of us, or only for me. And

maybe, probably, that doesn't matter. But I was listening intently to words about forgiveness when I
heard the following truth glistening new: that both
Peter and Judas were guilty of betraying Jesus—Peter
denied him three times with words; Judas led him into
the hands of his captors. And yet the greater sin of
Judas was *not* the dramatic act which precipitated
Christ's death. Nor was it his ultimate suicide. Rather it
was the *disbelief* which prompted his anguished taking
of his own life: his inability to accept the possibility of
God's total forgiveness. Judas couldn't believe, as Peter
could, that his deeds could be pardoned by Love.

Because we are all
betrayers, taking
silver and eating
body and blood and asking
(guilty) is it I and hearing
him say yes
it would be simple for us all
to rush out
and hang ourselves.

but if we find faith
to cry and wait
after the voice of morning
has crowed in our ears
clearly, enough
to break our hearts
he will be there
to ask us each again
Do you love me?[9]

Do we all carry Judas around inside? Our human sense of justice, of reward and punishment, is very strong, and we can't help feeling that terrible pain has to be the only satisfactory payment for great sin. Then we follow that assumption with the deeper, equally erroneous belief that no matter how great God's love, some sins must go beyond it; some mistakes *must* be unforgivable.

During my first year of community college counseling I grew very fond of a young, engaging student who often visited my office to chat. A number of months passed, however, before he told me about the enormous burden he'd been carrying.

When he was sixteen and had first received his driver's license he went out one evening with a few friends. He doesn't remember precisely how, but suddenly his car went out of control on a busy city street. He swerved into the curb and onto the sidewalk, instantly killing a young pedestrian.

No amount of kind words, sympathetic gestures, or reassurances had ever convinced him that he could be an "okay" person again. Within himself he believed that no forgiveness was wide enough to cover his deed. As Richard Bach has said, "Argue for your limitations and sure enough they're yours."[10] This boy argued. And the argument created a prison.

I still have sporadic contact with that young man. He has gone on to lead the life of one who is marked and guilty, for that is how he sees himself. He lives almost as if he were in hiding, but his flight cannot be achieved successfully; wherever he goes, he is there.

The circumstances of his accident were admittedly harsh and painful. But they have not bound him as tightly as he believes. It is he who has bound himself.

In order to accept the great gift of forgiveness we must begin by letting go. First I must let go of my notion that such forgiveness is in any sense deserved or earned (neither is possible), then I must let go of the possibility that forgiveness is ever denied the soul who seeks it. Such denial would be contrary to the very nature of the Forgiver. And finally, I must let go of the conviction that if I, personally, cannot imagine true forgiveness, it doesn't exist—a personal response that insults God, my neighbor, or whoever is willing to forgive me; a personal response that ends up enslaving me to my own stubborn guilt.

On earth wrong has to be punished. Err and you will suffer, we insist. But Divine Love lifts us unimaginably higher. Because of Christ, God's forgiveness can equal our wrong if we want it. That is God's majestic, "unnatural" equation.

As often as we insist upon guilt, punishment, and payment, we resist the rules of Love's realm.

Of course I am speaking here of the *inner* land of heart and soul, and not of judgment, for example, by a jury, or a teacher, or a parent. Human systems of justice attempt to make the world safe, orderly, rational. I am not advocating the abolition of law or discipline. My concern is with the judgments which spring from within human hearts and which go on punishing and withholding love long after civil systems of justice have meted out their penalties.

We need to think seriously and deeply about this and guard ourselves against ever feeling justified in withholding love and forgiveness, even from ourselves.

Here is a tough blanket statement: We are never justified in withholding love. How can God's way be so outrageously demanding? Only because its counter-offer, bought with Christ's blood, is true—that whatever wrong we will ever do has already been wiped clean and forgiven and his cleansing *can*, with our believing, be made real within us. Total forgiveness, nothing less, is reality in God. Why do we fail to believe it? Why do we readily believe less?

Now, try these other questions:

Do you or I wait to believe and accept a truth only after we've seen a need for it? What if I fail to see my own need of being forgiven because I view myself as innocent of sins against the law, but fail to see my guilt about the sins Jesus called more serious—sins like selfishness, pride, hypocrisy, shallowness, prejudice, uselessness, withholding love?

What is it that causes us to hurl stones at Love? Why are we so consistent in pushing away what we need the most? Why are we so reluctant to believe what is wonderful?

Maybe it's because of a deeper question—asked of me not only in countless letters, but also in many a receiving line or casual conversation. "Where is God?"

I pray, people tell me, but God remains silent. I beg for help, but it doesn't come. I asked for A, and I got B. Why does he answer other pleas, but not mine? How is it that I pray and pray and pray and things get worse?

How do you find God? These are the questions.

In every one of our beginnings, I do believe, we were created with a magnificent entity known as a will. (I don't know why. To know why is to be God, or to be as large as his mind, isn't it? If that's right, then I can go on to assume that no one else knows why either.) The simple fact is, God gave us the freedom to choose the course of our own lives.

Many theologians (who must be cringing that I'd have the temerity to even touch this subject) suppose that we were given freedom to choose because love which is freely given has infinitely greater meaning and value. That makes sense to my human mind, but I still don't see how we can know for sure that it was the intent of God.

In his powerful essay "It Was God's Will," Sheldon Vanauken expands this theory. He imagines life as it would be if it were devoid of any act which has been generated freely. In Vanauken's piece God steps in (as we so often angrily blame him for *not* doing), and disallows every negative thought, and every harmful act:

A Nazi guard turns a handle to start the gas flowing in upon the huddled victims behind the heavy glass. He yawns. He's done this so many times. No thrill left. Then he notices that the people in the chamber are not clawing their throats. Odd. He gives the handle another push, just as the walls of the gas chamber dissolve. He and the other guards snatch out pistols and fire. God catches the bullets in his hand.

A submarine fires a spread of torpedoes. It appears that two at least will strike the cruiser, and 800 men will die, including one family's three fine sons. God reaches into the water and' seizes the torpedoes. The proud cruiser steams on.

A rapist is leering down at his terrified victim. Then he finds an invisible wall between him and her.

A woman screaming at her tired husband, as she has done for years, is suddenly voiceless. A boy's cruel epithet flung at a high school girl who would be scarred by it is heard by no one.

All this—it's right nice, isn't it? This is the God we want, we think. We are ready to reelect God, God. But let us look further.

You cannot shoot anybody, but also—since God can't draw lines—you cannot bark at your wife or cheat on your income tax. The fist cannot connect. The cruel word cannot be said. Free will has been repealed. No one now chooses to be good; he *must* be.

Newspapers shrink. No more wars or rumors of war . . . Almost every novel ever written will soon come to seem unreal, for they were about a world where good guys strove with bad ones, and courage meant something. And goodness . . .

The gift God gave to man was the freedom to choose. If God acts to prevent the consequences of choice, the gift is withdrawn. . . . For awhile people will wistfully yearn to hurt somebody, but new generations will have forgotten choice.

To finite man, what meaning can *goodness* have if there is no badness? . . . God's grand experiment of creating people free to love and trust Him or to hate Him will be all over. We, compelled to be good, not choosing, shall sink into apathy... We who are created for the stars.[11]

But in the end, even these speculations are futile. Life is as it is. We cannot alter it. And so we must decide to fight it or accept it. Only in accepting it do we go on to learn more.

If we can agree that we are given free wills, then we walk straight into the second common cry that I hear: How can a God of love allow such dire consequences as freedom breeds? The question is tricky because half of it is falsely assumed: that God's idea of love is just like mine. And my idea of love is goodness, happiness, and the absence of pain.

But I'm not so sure that definition also belongs to God. I think of physical relief and comfort, temporary wants and desires. I believe he cares about these too, but *less* than he cares about the state of my soul which has permanent value, and less than he cares about my real, inner growth. Or yours.

The view from the inside of me tells me that no God of love can possibly take pleasure in watching suffering unfold. He cannot sit without feeling when he knows a child suffers or is abused. He cannot be compassionless when he sees that any man or woman is frightened, lonely, or sick. He cannot be uncaring as we bear secret burdens which seem too great to bear. But all such sufferings results from personal freedom, the freedom he gave. They are consequences of freedom wrongly used. And if he were to interrupt that, he would interrupt the order of the universe which he has established. Interrupting this order must in some sense not be right.

The more fruitful question is, I think, that given this awesome freedom, how can we live well? What is it to really love? Not glamorous, romantic, movie-star love. But real love which is its own answer, and requires no return in order to be fulfilling. Love which has no boundary. Love which gives us the inner steel to transcend all attempts to defeat us.

Ironically, *that* is the stuff of life. Not cars. Not clothes. Nor careers. Not money. Not even families. Love may include these, but it outdistances them all.

But my detractors will have more arguments. And yes, I do know that in history's course God has, at times, stepped in. And many could accept the authority of free will, whatever it is, until this issue of God's seeming favoritism arises. Mary's child lies sick and dying. Her family, friends, and church pray for the child to live. And she does. She is cured, beyond explanation. A miracle. God intervened.

Now Carol's child lies sick and dying. Her family, friends, and church pray for the child to live. And she doesn't. There is no cure. No miracle. No intervention.

I have lived in the depths of this argument because I was a Carol. And the human question can't help but burst from every Carol's heart: Why? It isn't fair. How can God choose one weeping mother over another, or one suffering patient, or one lonely person?

Such despair is followed by a search for formulas. Mary's miracle can be yours if you pray *this* prayer. If you use *this* ointment. If you visit *this* shrine. If you have *this* many people praying. If you *really* believe. If you never doubt.

Such solutions are tricky, again, because they cover another false assumption. They assume that there is a way for humans to control God and force him to intervene. That there is a magic formula. But if we can control him, then is he God?

And isn't fairness a human term, defined in finite ways, perceived with human eyes and hearts, and thus limited, very limited? God is not just a super human. He is himself; his fairness and his justice are divine, eternal. His justice takes *all* things into account, things we can't know, even the most brilliant of us.

I think I have learned at last to be comfortable with God being God. I accept him as such and I don't try too hard to comprehend what my mind can't possibly know. He asks for love and worship, not comprehension of his Godship. I do not ask him to measure up to *my* idea of what is fair and right. I ask him to stretch me, to enlarge my concept of him, to trust *his* fairness even without full sight of it.

In Mary's hour of tears he saw and he knew. And in that instance, for his own reasons, he intervened and brought life and joy.

In Carol's (and my own) hour of tears he saw and knew. And in that instance, for his own reasons, he did not intervene. He allowed the pain.

I know he heard both sets of prayers and was moved by them. He loved every individual in each situation. But the *why* is his, not mine.

Still another hard question follows: If God is not controlled by prayer, isn't it therefore useless to pray? Won't he do what he is going to do anyway? So why bother?

At first glance that seems to be a rational response. But beware of first glances, especially when you hurt. Prayer is pointless only if its sole purpose is to attain our own specific demands. But is that its purpose?

Prayer, in simplest definition, is communication with God. And the most perfect intent of mature prayer is not to receive what we desire, but to find God's will for us. How do I know? Christ modeled it with his own life: "My Father, if it is possible, may this cup be taken from me. Yet not as I will but as you will."

Many answers are found there. First, of course we are to petition. "Please, take this cup..." How else can we communicate but by speaking? And so we ask in the same simple way that we would with any friend. In friendship the more frequently and deeply we talk and listen, the better we come to know each other, the closer a friend that other becomes. And so it is with God; it is no different.

A true friend, God will always be moved by our needs. He will always care; he will always want to know, and if it's right (based on his perfect, full knowledge) he'll change things. And if it's not right, he'll change *us*, as long as we're willing. He can only transform an open heart.

In the long run God's will must be best. But the proof of that cannot simply be our feelings, our under-standing, or our convictions. Our sight is human, limited, and we are small. The proof and measure of God's love is Christ's assurance of it. To depend upon any other sign may lead us astray. Feelings and miracles are not the sole signs of God's presence, nor are lack of feelings and miracles signs of his absence. He is defined

by no measure other than the truth that he is. Always.
And always Love.

Thus walking closer to God demands our acceptance
of ourselves as less, and him as greater. It encompasses
the unanswered whys about free will and pain, and the
sought, but sometimes not received, interventions. It
encompasses every moment of pain and horror which is
allowed.

Finally—the most painful question of all—how may
we understand the abuse or molestation of a young
child? (And other horrors, maybe.) But how could a
God of love ever allow such damage to a helpless victim? How could he know and not act to prevent?

I don't know. I have to say that first—I don't know.
And it's caught up and is a part of my not knowing how
he could allow many things. It's part of his first allowing freedom. It flows naturally from that.

But it's fruitless then to conclude, "I will have nothing to do with a God who allows such pain." That conclusion leads to no real resolution, and so there must be
a better conclusion to draw. It is an impasse for me to
confront this issue and only end up discrediting God.
Since he's the greater of the two of us, I've asked him to
teach me to search deeper, for better answers. I need to
dig so deeply that if anyone is to risk being discredited,
it's I.

I remember a young woman who once tearfully recounted to me a series of painful childhood abuses
which had left her deeply scarred. The unanswered
question which continually haunted her was, "How
could God stand by and not help me when I was so
helpless?"

Part of her answer lies back in that unknowable arena of when and why God sometimes intervenes and sometimes does not. But it also touches upon something more. In our haste to blame God for his failure to prevent all misfortunes, we may very well err and blame him, too, for omissions which are not his, but ours.

Maybe the proper question to wrestle with instead is: Just what is a church?

Does that seem strange? The idea of a church has relevance here, for *we* are the channel through which God most often works to bring about goodness and love. And being a follower and a channel along with other followers and channels, is what it means to me to be a church.

That means that if I cry to God in despair and loneliness, he will often respond to me by prompting the heart of another person who is able to fill my need. He might weave into this person's thinking the impulse, "Drop in and see Paula this morning." Or, "Give Paula a call." Or a friend, driving past my home, may suddenly feel compelled to turn the car and drive in.

Thus the body of Christ. The church. People loving and caring for other people. Obviously if someone seeks these suggestions from God, indeed listens for them, he will hear them more often, and recognize them more readily. And whomever this listener visits or helps will feel inclined to say, "God really heard my prayer and didn't abandon me. Someone came."

But far too often the converse is true. Someone prays and cries in need. And God sees another person, or body of people (a church) who might fill that need, and tries to reach these other hearts so that they will carry

his love. But the individual or group does not respond
—they're too busy, their lives are already too complete,
and so they push away their inclinations to help others.
Or they may feel too burdened themselves, and so
think only of their own pain. The excuses are many. But
the point is clear: When no aid comes to the crying
person it is not God who has abandoned him. He will
not. He cannot. But a fellow human can, and often
does. We are all guilty.

I don't know the full circumstances of that scarred
young woman's early childhood. I know she was
abused and not rescued. But I ask myself is it possible
that God could have seen her plight and not have
cared? I *know* he could not. I am sure he felt her pain
and anguished over it, and I would venture that he tried
and tried to move and open the eyes of someone within
her life who might have rescued her. I would guess that
he tried relentlessly. But men, in their freedom to
choose, chose to look the other way, and did. Maybe
they were all too busy, or too unconcerned, or hurting
themselves.

Where are we left? God gave us freedom and saw
how hurtfully we used it. He watched us court our own
destruction. If he damned us without recourse it would
deny his all-forgiving love. But to leave our evil choices
undealt with would deny his all-perfect justice. Christ
was the perfect resolution. Becoming man, he paid our
penalty.

I think that as he stood at the foot of his own cross he
saw all human life, past and future. I believe he saw
that scarred young woman, then unborn, who spoke so

tearfully to me. He saw the pain a man's free choice would inflict on her over and over again. He saw the others God would try to impel to help her. He saw their closed hearts and busy minds. He saw how they would choose to ignore. He saw her, finally, alone and fearful amid churches and people who spoke of, but did not know, Love.

He saw that in this future instance God would not intervene. In Gethsemane, the night before, he had not intervened either. He knew that this girl would be forced to endure her horror.

And he could change only one thing. By allowing himself to be strung upon the cross he could remove the power of that pain to defeat that child. He could prevent it from having the final say. He could open the door to the healing of her tears if she would ever come to him. He could open the door to another life without pain.

And I believe, seeing her, seeing all the children, the men, women, all of us, he offered his hand to the bloody bite of the nail, his side to the slice of the sword. He gave his whole life. What more was there?

Every cry of humanity was heard and died for at that cross. The comfort is left to flow through us as hands and arms of Christ.

And yet we must acknowledge one thing more. Christ also knew at the foot of that cross that in years to come, in spite of all of this—the incarnation, the trauma, millions of those for whom he'd done it wouldn't care or understand. In fact they would *blame* him for their pain and dare to speak of his lack of love and caring. They would not see the human beings who'd let them down. They would say that *he* had abandoned them.

That knowledge, I think, must have hurt him more than the nail and the spear. Even so, he accepted it.

And that is the God whom I know and with whom I walk. And that is why I obey him.

These are my hard-won conclusions. Everyone will find them if they question and ache as I have. They're from my head and they're from my heart. They're from my struggles to walk away from a blood-stained highway by myself and not forever hate life and its author. They're from my longing to make something good of my life. They're from my longing to have something worthy to offer back to all those lives who sustained me when I was hurting and unable to think, living so far away in the grief-filled realm of the emotions.

But all of these thoughts put together, even with me holding them out to you, are still philosophy and theology. And when a human heart is breaking, my thoughts, my conclusions will not be enough. Life will need to go way beyond them.

Ultimately it is strong arms, the answering tears, the touch of another hand which makes the unbearable bearable, and which quiets the question, "Why?"

AFTERWORD

I feel two thoughts at once: I feel as if I've said all I can, and at the same time as if I've only just begun, that I haven't *really* started to say it, and that makes me shudder. Maybe there's no difference between the first chapter and the last.

So the middle is what counts. That's where we live. That's the dark, mysterious spot between God's promise of life and his answer. That's the spot where we need to figure out the richest use of our human gifts, never denying what makes us ourselves. That's the spot where the human, changed by the divine, is sanctified. The danger is that that's also the spot where we may sin, compromising ourselves and wishing to be other than where or who we are. And that's where we kill the spirit in others, or exalt one expression of beauty or human gift at the expense of others, to the exclusion of God.

It's in the middle that we feel most tempted to give up. To throw it all in at the eleventh hour, when we always *feel* the furthest from the goal but when really we are the closest. That's where it matters that we know that the power of defeat is in our own hearts, and that our disbelieving self, not circumstances, is the enemy. That's where it matters that we give power to our dreams, arms and legs to our love, wings to our wonder, so that they will become the significant part of us.

I fear the day that technology and science convince us that all is knowable. Or that how we live is not what matters, or that the key to loving rests in our knowledge and our capabilities, and not in our hearts and wills.

I shrink from coming to think that we are not responsible for all our actions, and answers. That morality has to do with our adherence to strict, abstract standards, and not with how we treat other people.

What contrast—life and death! We've made one good and one evil. In pain and joy, happiness and tears, we've created polar opposites, and that's an illusion.

So I repeat my original conclusions, and leave them with you in the form of questions: Is a tear only sadness, or can it be joy as well? Does the wind sometimes blow things down? Is God still love, then? Can I understand joy without understanding sorrow? Do they separate, even inside of me? Can I understand life, and not accept its author? To whom or what *am* I holding on? Who owns me? What limitations have become my prison?

Where does the wind begin? (Answer for yourself; I cannot do your searching for you.) And when you have decided, turn, and go where it goes.

Pneuma
" . . . so it is with the Spirit." John 3:8

The wind breathes where it wishes.
The wind blows where it blows.

A flurry of starlings
scatter like lifted leaves
across the dark October field
driven against
their own warm, southward
impulse: winged instinct

thwarted by
a weight of wind.

The eye of Your storm
sees from the wild height.
Your air augments the world,
tearing
away dead wood, testing,
toughening all trees,
spreading all seeds,
thawing a winter wasteland,
sifting the sand, carving
the rock, the water,
in the end
moving the mountain.

Your wind breathes where it wishes,
moves where it wills, sometimes
severs my safe moorings. Sovereign gusts—
buffet my wings with your blowing,
loosen me, lift me to go
wherever you're going. [12]

NOTES

1. New York: Random House, 1975.
2. Psalm 63:1, 8.
3. Matthew 25:44-45.
4. Charles Doss, *I Shall Mingle* (self-published).
5. Hugh Prather, *Notes to Myself* (Moab, Utah: Real People Press, 1970).
6. *Time for God* (Nashville: Abingdon Press, 1967), p. 13.
7. Paula D'Arcy, *Song for Sarah* (Wheaton, Ill.: Harold Shaw Publishers, 1979), pp. 52-53.
8. Luci Shaw, "Behind the Walls," *The Secret Trees* (Wheaton, Ill.: Harold Shaw Publishers, 1976), p. 11.
9. Luci Shaw, "Judas, Peter," *The Sighting* (Wheaton, Ill.: Harold Shaw Publishers, 1981), p. 82.
10. Richard Bach, *Illusions* (New York: Delacorte Press, 1977), p. 75.
11. "It Was God's Will," *The Living Church*, 21 June 1981, p. 137.
12. Luci Shaw, "Pneuma," *The Secret Trees* (Wheaton, Ill.: Harold Shaw Publishers, 1976), p. 62.